Just Looking and Other Essays

Other books by Helen McLean

Significant Things (2003)
(Finalist, 2004 Commonwealth Prize for Best Book,
Canada and Caribbean division)

Details From a Larger Canvas (2001)

Of All the Summers (1998)

Sketching From Memory,
a Portrait of My Mother (1994)

With my very good wishes to Jay & Linda from Helen

Just Looking
AND OTHER ESSAYS

by

Helen McLean

Seraphim Editions

Just Looking, Unmet Friends and *Elevation* have appeared in *Room of One's Own; Second Sight* and *Life Study* in *Ars Medica; Speaking Italian Like a Canadian* in *Accenti Magazine*.

Italicized passages in *Life Study* are quoted from *A Patient's Guide to Hip Replacement* with the kind permission of Medical Multimedia Group LLC, 228 West Main St., Suite D, Missoula, Montana, 59802.

Lines of poetry in *Life Study* are quoted from W. H. Auden's *Letter to Lord Byron*, in *W.H. Auden Collected Poems*, edited by Edward Mendelson, Faber & Faber, London, 1991, page 100.

The publisher gratefully acknowledges the financial assistance of the Canada Council for the Arts and the Ontario Arts Council.

**Canada Council Conseil des Arts
for the Arts du Canada**

**ONTARIO ARTS COUNCIL
CONSEIL DES ARTS DE L'ONTARIO**

Library and Archives Canada Cataloguing in Publication

McLean, Helen
    Just looking : and other essays / by Helen McLean.

Includes bibliographical references.
ISBN 978-0-9808879-2-1

    1. McLean, Helen. 2. Painters–Canada–Biography. 3. Authors, Canadian (English)–20th century–Biography. I. Title.

ND249.M286A2 2008   759.11   C2008-901899-0

Editor: Tanya Nanavati
Cover Painting: Helen McLean
Author Photo: Ross McLean
Cover Design and Typography: Julie McNeill, McNeill Design Arts

Published in 2008 by
Seraphim Editions
238 Emerald St. N.
Hamilton, ON
Canada L8L 5K8

Printed and bound in Canada

For Simon

Contents

Just Looking

I come with my dog to the old brickworks park in the Don River Valley several times a month, in all seasons and weathers, to walk and to look. It is a place of delight. Limestone and clay were once cut and mined from this basin to build the metropolis rising around it, but late in the last century, after its resources had been exhausted, the city undertook to restore the scarred landscape and transform it into a mid-Toronto sanctuary where indigenous creatures and native plants might prosper. A tributary of the Don pours into a series of large contiguous ponds and wetlands that are connected to each other by wooden walkways and bridges. Footpaths wind through acres of meadow that in summer are strewn with wildflowers; on the hillsides clumps of flowering shrubs and stands of poplar and cedar have taken hold. The park seethes with life. Sharp-eyed herons stand motionless in the marshes waiting for schools of little fish to come their way; striped snails inch their way insouciantly across footpaths onto which even the occasional garter snake will risk emerging from the tall grass to sun itself. In winter muskrats venture from their thatchy bulrush houses in the ponds and leave trails of dainty footprints in the snow. When spring arrives this sheltered valley resonates with birdsong.

Sheba, a German Shepherd, has keen senses. Her interest in the place is instinctual. She trots ahead along the path, looking from side to side, casing the landscape. Is there a squirrel or low-flying bird to chase or another dog to romp with? She stops suddenly, retraces her steps, cocks an ear to the ground to listen to a mouse scurrying under the leaves. She raises her nose to catch the scent of some creature, perhaps a fox, that passed by recently. For me it's not so simple.

It has been said that there is no such thing as "just looking," because the eye is constantly searching for an object. But it is not the eye that searches, it's the mind. The eye is an innocent recorder that gives no more weight to one thing than to another. It witnesses what's in range — pond, bulrushes, trees, sky — all of a piece, as flat shapes and colours and tones. Then the mind immediately begins to scan what the eye reports, sorts it all into categories, layers things as to depth and perspective, chooses in a flash what it will attend to and what it will ignore, and names everything in sight.

Sheba's eye skips the pond and the flora and fauna in the foreground and fastens on a squirrel halfway up a tree trunk off to the distant right. I look at the same scene and my brain hurtles into search mode, coming up in split seconds with *red-winged blackbird* (kindergarten book pored over seven decades ago), *early returning migrant*, (personal observation site), while a field guide consulted now and then over the years

supplies *nests in wetlands,* and *colouring indicates this one's a male.* Still unsatisfied, my mind classifies some yellow flowers near the pond — *mustard, member of the cruciferae family* (high school botany) — hunts for a term to describe the sky and comes up with an artist's colour, *cerulean.* All this cerebral activity rapidly diminishes the direct perception of what is before my eyes, and by the time the brain has finished its busy interfering work I have pretty well ceased to see anything at all. Becoming aware of oneself as observer is the death of observation. Oh, I can still see the landscape, but it has separated itself into parts that can't be put together again. The scene has ceased to be a whole. I have particularized it to death.

I brought a visitor from Calgary to the valley one day. She was amazed to find a large park right in the centre of the city.

"It's like Central Park in New York," she said.

I stared at her. "They're both parks," I said, "but there the resemblance ends."

"I don't mean it *looks* like Central Park, it *is* like Central Park," she said, fishing a small camera out of her shoulder bag and putting it to her eye.

My mind can't stop supplying me with dry facts that I don't want to hear about and my friend was unable to accept what was before her eyes without comparing it to something better-known and more important. The photographs she was taking would only be symbols of what was there, no more able to reveal the truth about the park than the word "mustard" revealed the truth about the flower. But how do you put the brakes on the brain? The only way I know of recovering that first unfractured gestalt is to attempt to translate it into paint and canvas, to make a material object that bridges the space between what is before my eyes and what I know about its parts. If I'm successful it will reflect the scene in a new form, with everything knitted back together again so solidly that you couldn't pry that blackbird or those yellow flowers loose with a crowbar.

A painting is not a record of what is there but a record of seeing it. On a visit to Paris one summer I stood transfixed in front of a painting by Claude Monet, a scene composed of a few trees, a patch of sky, a substantial country house of red brick, and in the foreground a flock of white turkeys pecking about in the grass. It is midsummer, hot. The time of day appears to be early morning. The sky is a nacreous blue-pink, the house looks closed and silent, as though everyone were still asleep. Sunlight lies in yellow streaks across part of the blue-shadowed grass, backlighting in pale gold the fanned-out tail feathers of a male turkey in the midst of the flock. The carmine of the birds' wattles vibrates against the shadowy blue-green grass and the white plumage that the artist has rendered in shades of pale violet and blue. The bodies of nine of the birds are either contiguous or overlapping; one loner is off to the right, and the head and neck of another rise in the immediate foreground from the bottom of the picture frame, its bright eye on the viewer. A distant group of the birds is brushed in so loosely that only the context identifies them as turkeys at all. The painting has about it a quality of silence. It glows with meaning. I have little interest in domestic fowl, grass is grass and I've seen lots of brick houses — but then what I was looking at was none of these. What held and transported me was not birds and grass, but a ravishingly beautiful work of art.

In my earlier days I didn't know whether my reaction to what I saw and how I felt about it were universal phenomena or just something peculiar to me. Like my friend who wanted to certify the park's significance by comparing it with other parks, I went searching in the writings of other people to validate my responses to the visible world, and perhaps find an explanation for the feelings of timelessness and the loss of the sense of self that seemed to be part and parcel of the business of seeing.

I was familiar with the writing of C. S. Lewis through his witty *Screwtape Letters*, and now I was drawn to his autobiography by its title *Surprised by Joy* which seemed to describe certain moments of my own life. I knew I was on the right track when he said the enjoyment of something and the contemplation of that enjoyment are incompatible, that the surest way of spoiling a pleasure is to start examining your satisfaction in it because the minute you start observing yourself you cease to observe what's before your eyes.

Lewis described occasional but unforgettable moments of ecstatic joy he'd felt in the early years of his life, a time that he later realized was characterized by a marked absence of beauty. "No picture on the walls of my father's house ever attracted — and indeed none deserved — our attention. We never saw a beautiful building nor imagined that a building could be beautiful." Then, when he was still a little boy, his brother showed him a toy garden he'd created of moss and flowers in the lid of a biscuit tin, the first thing he had ever seen that he recognized as beautiful. "As long as I live," he wrote, "my imagination of Paradise will retain something of my brother's toy garden."

Later, in another house, standing near some currant bushes in fragrant bloom, the memory of that miniature garden came back to him, and he was suddenly transported into a realm of enormous bliss that he was at a loss to find words powerful enough to describe. It seemed at the time like a kind of desire, a longing, but it vanished so quickly that all he was left with was a longing for the longing, and a sense of the moment's incalculable importance. Everything else that had ever happened to him was insignificant in comparison. "It was something quite different from ordinary life and even from ordinary pleasure; something, as they would now say, 'in another dimension,'" and although he has described the sensation as 'longing,' he then goes on to say that the very nature of that longing "makes nonsense of our common distinction between having and wanting." Lewis said he tried without success to pursue that ephemeral feeling by concentrating and preparing his mind for it to come again, until he realized at last that those experiences could never be summoned but had to be awaited, patiently, with an attitude of passive receptiveness. He recommended this same passive attitude toward art, too, saying that preferring and comparing does little good when we are dealing with works of art and endless harm when we are dealing with nature. We must shut our mouths and open our eyes and ears and give ourselves up to total surrender.

I wondered if the experiences Lewis described and that were so like my own were just some sort of psychic short circuit or if they might have a more profound or even a religious significance. One book led to another. From *The Variety of Religious Experience* I learned that William James categorized episodes like these as mystical in nature, modes of feeling rather than of thought. He wrote that everyone who underwent them reported certain common characteristics — a sense of having encountered a reality more real than the everyday, and of "being at-one with everything in the world in a rapturous loss of self." All this echoed what I felt myself. If I had been pressed to describe the emotion those moments aroused in me I would have borrowed a phrase I remembered from my churchgoing youth and said it was like "the peace which passeth all understanding."

In a memoir, *Sketching From Memory*, I wrote about the sense of timelessness that sometimes seemed to descend on me out of nowhere. I had heard that a traveller in a hot air balloon feels no wind in the face and no sensation of motion because the voyager is at one with the currents of air. My transcendent moments similarly appeared to take place in a bubble of nowness that either moved with time, like the balloon in the wind, or had nothing to do with it at all. Those moments were not related to charming vistas or the faces of loved ones. One soggy day in January, when I was walking through the little park at the foot of my street, I felt myself moving into that silent bubble of suspended time, a complete and utter sense of the *now*. I stopped in my tracks and stood there with my heels sinking into the cold mud, suddenly aware of the utter beauty of everything before my eyes and of my certain knowledge that everything was all right, that everything was just as it ought to be.

Would Lewis's "joy" be beyond the capacity of one who could neither see nor hear? I sat beside a man on a bus travelling from Toronto to Peterborough one summer evening, a two-hour trip during which he told me had been born deaf and had completely lost his sight as a small child. He had never learned to speak, but we conversed; he by writing in a little notebook and passing it over for me to read; I by writing words letter by letter in the palm of his hand with my forefinger. At one point he took my two hands in his and taught me how to form the letters of the alphabet. He had a job at the Institute for the Blind, he told me, but he was also a sculptor. He modeled animals in clay, was working on a lobster at the time. He was off to spend the weekend with a couple who had a house by a lake, where he would swim and go out with them in their boat. He loved the smell of pine trees. Who could say that his dark and silent world was without moments of ecstasy?

When one is wide-eyed, really looking, "all eyes" in the same sense that one can be "all ears," there is a crucial instant before the brain starts analysing a scene and sorting out its components. In that millisecond the vista in the Don Valley Park is grasped all at once as shapes on a single plane in which the edge of one object meets the edge of the next — bulrush shape, bird shape, water shape, tree shape, sky shape — like pieces of a jigsaw puzzle fitted together. It is that moment I want to capture. From quick drawings made on the spot I will later develop a composition, and on that framework I may, just may, succeed in making a painting that will have the quality, in senses both temporal and physical, of "presentness."

Until the way to do it was finally worked out during the Renaissance, artists had been trying for centuries to make realistic-looking representations of a three-dimensional world on a two-dimensional surface. By the middle of the twentieth century the process was thrown into reverse. The influential critic Harold Rosenberg, who coined the expression "action painting," said post-war abstract expressionism was the culmination, the supreme flowering of western art and figurative painting was a thing of the past.

Then the equally influential critic Clement Greenberg came along and announced that the open loose brushwork of action painting had to be scrapped too, because it could, and frequently did, give a feeling of airiness and spatial depth, which meant that a bird or an airplane could *fly* between those great black brushstrokes of Franz Kline's, for example. Jackson Pollock's drip paintings passed muster because ground and figure were so inextricably tangled that a bird could no more fly through them than a mosquito fly through a Brillo pad. A couple of other exceptions managed to slide under the wire: figurative work was permissable if what was represented were itself already two-dimensional, like the image of a printed comic strip, and optical illusion could be allowed on the grounds that the illusion of a third dimension takes place not in the work of art but on the viewer's retina.

All other forms of representation were to be banished. Any indication of a third dimension in painting was the province of sculpture, Greenberg said, and not in painting's bailiwick at all, so even the outline of something as innocuous as a teacup would suggest the cup's volume, and there you were right back into the illusion of depth again. There could be no more painting that gave the viewer the feeling he was looking into the proscenium of a stage; painting must compress the stage until the backdrop was on the same plane as the curtain. The canvas and the marks the artist made on it had not only to be on the same plane, which of course they were, but must also *appear* to be. Period.

By the time I got around to reading Greenberg's *Art and Culture* during the mid-sixties I had already read and heard his catchphrase about the unbreachable integrity of the picture-plane more times than enough. *Says who?* The idea of setting out to make a purely abstract painting, putting brush to canvas without first having an image in the mind's eye, has always seemed to me like taking scissors to cloth without knowing what the garment was to be, but in those days declaring yourself unpersuaded by Greenberg's arguments concerning the overwhelming importance of the flat ground was like arguing for creationism versus evolution.

I'd always thought the critic's job was to comment upon and evaluate what was being done in the present, but here was Greenberg dictating what painting ought to be in the future. Some of his comments in *Art and Culture* had a hysterical ring to them; I visualized him as Daumier's little clown waving his fists in the air, demanding to be heard, full of sound and fury and little else. From what I saw during occasional visits to New York, the increasingly bloated scale of these non-figurative works failed to compensate for their lack of content. I didn't get it, I couldn't understand why anyone listened to Greenberg at all, but almost everyone did, and his pronouncements affected the schools, the art markets, the museums and galleries, and just about every working artist in North America and beyond. For painters who were weak at drawing and pedestrian in their ideas anyway the switch-over to abstraction was a bonanza, but many figurative painters of authentic talent had either to climb aboard the abstraction bandwagon or find their work sidelined as old fashioned and passé.

One who held out was Fairfield Porter, an artist whose work I love. He was a contemporary of Kline and Pollock and found himself caught up in the controversy but underwent a crucial moment of decision when he saw an exhibition of the works of post-Impressionist painters Pierre Bonnard and Edouard Vuillard. He made up his mind to paint what he knew and what he saw around him — the Maine landscape, figures, and interiors of the house he lived in with his wife and children — and let the painting speak for itself. Private means allowed him to be independent of the approbation of the critics and the convulsions of the New York art scene and perfectly free to ignore Greenberg's decree that it was impossible to paint the figure any more.

Porter said he found the energy of a painting in the substance of the paint itself, and in his work a patch of fog or a splash of sunlight are given the same weight as trees and hill. If occasionally an object seems almost to be dissolving into transparency, like the sun-blasted wicker armchair in his painting of a screened porch, it is not because he denies the solidity of the chair but because the real subject of the work is the dazzle of light, and everything else is but a vehicle to support it. Porter tried not to see the various objects in the round as they actually were, he said, but to see only where one thing ended and another began. He described a quality in a painting that he called "presence," something akin to the presence a child feels and recognizes in the things he sees, and believed a work of art is only successful when the viewer recognizes this presence too. He said he used to feel, not unpleasantly, that the inanimate objects he painted had an awareness of him, that they *knew*.

Some years ago I saw an exhibition of the work of Giorgio Morandi at the Tate Gallery in London and came out walking into walls. Morandi painted meticulously composed still-life arrangements of unremarkable household objects and views of the equally unremarkable landscape near Grizzana where he spent his summers. He also made a few studies of what he could see from the window of the small room he used as a studio, in the Bologna apartment he shared all his life with his three unmarried sisters. The paintings at the Tate were so intensely real, so compellingly solid and full of presentness that when I left the gallery and went out into London's wan afternoon, the streets and buildings and even the people looked pallid and diffuse and half-transparent.

A few days later I saw a tiny Morandi painting, scarcely bigger than a postcard, for sale in a gallery on Cork Street. I enquired about the price, backed quickly out of the gallery and walked down to Hatchard's Bookshop in Piccadilly, where I bought Karen Wilkin's beautifully illustrated book about the artist instead. In *Giorgio Morandi* Wilkin writes that she has been tempted to use a response to Morandi's work as a partial measure — among artists and non-artists alike — of the ability to see. She believes the driving force behind his work was the sheer power of a scrutiny so passionate that it could wrest deep feeling from unevocative subject matter. Morandi once told a friend he was glad he wasn't obliged to deal with what he called the modern dilemma, and he paid no attention to the critics or the passing fashions in art. All his life he painted simplified forms from nature and from his humdrum collection of still-life objects, revelling, Wilkin says, in their particular shapes and in the substance of paint itself.

The relationship between Morandi and his collection of flea-market pantry utensils — small boxes and bowls, an olive-oil can, pitchers, bottles and carafes of various shapes, a fluted thing that might be a lemon-reamer — was intense. He removed the labels from the bottles and covered them in flat paint to eliminate reflection, then left all this domestic detritus on the shelves in his studio until a thick layer of dust gathered on them, which gave a certain unity to his limited palette of buffs, blues, browns, grays, white, and accents of black. His arrangements are frontal and formal, set in shallow pictorial depth and bathed in a clear light. These objects, like Porter's porch and armchair, were the armatures for Morandi's lifelong investigation of the possibilities of paint, but he also infused them with a kind of breathing, trembling energy that exudes self-awareness and a mysterious significance. They *know*.

Morandi said that nothing could be more abstract, more unreal, than appearances, that the material world never really exists as we see and understand it. We accommodate to that unreality by attaching meanings to things, giving them names, sorting them into categories — cup, lobster, bottle, chair — as a way of taming them and absorbing them into our lives so we can more or less cease to notice them.

On a dull winter afternoon in what must have been my seventh year I was alone in the living room of our house when a beam of low sunlight broke through the clouds and shot through the tall front window, piercing the darkness of the room. It was the sort of shaft of light that in a Baroque painting would be beaming an angel down to earth or lighting the way for the Virgin's assumption into heaven. This ray contained no human form but it was full of dust motes, a tube of them, glittering like diamonds suspended in gelatin, that stretched across the room from the window to the floor. I followed the slanted ray with my astounded eyes and saw that where it landed the old red carpet was on fire. It may have been the eye-peeling moment when mere seeing was replaced by a lifelong addiction to looking.

I stand at the edge of one of the ponds in the brickworks park, looking down to watch a school of little dappled brown fish dart in and out of the reeds. Out of the corner of my eye I catch a sudden streak of blue slicing downward through the bright green, flashing past the reflection of sunlit foliage and plummeting into white clouds. I quickly name it — kingfisher. A man standing on the wooden bridge across the end of the pond goes into a shimmy-and-shake as a breeze stirs the water. The weather, the time of day and the changing seasons alter everything from one moment to the next. When you are addicted to looking you are forever being thrown off balance, shaken up, transported. There's no keeping up with it. You need eyes in the back of your head.

Interior with a Dog

To enter a space where light and air are beautifully contained within walls of right and lovely proportions is a sublime aesthetic experience. Great palaces and cathedrals may be transporting, but smaller interiors can gladden the heart too. It doesn't do to love one's house too much — or anything else in the material world, for that matter — but the house I live in now has been more pleasing to me than any of the others I've inhabited so far. In the library one day my eye fell upon a book about the architecture and writings of Frank Lloyd Wright, and I brought it home to find out what it was that made a house more than a roof over the head. After looking at pictures of some of the houses he designed I wondered what he might think of my three-storey Victorian semi, with one neighbour smack dab against its south wall and another across a narrow driveway to the north.

After reading Wright's criteria for the good house, though, I decided mine would qualify on several counts, maybe even all of them. He said that in a good house form does not merely follow function, they are indivisibly one, and that the parts of the house are to its whole as the whole is to the part, related in a logical way, like trunk and branch and twig of a tree. He believed that the outer shell of the house should reflect its inner spaces rather than the other way around, that it must be in harmony with its setting and in keeping with the times in which it is built. Size and proportion of the good house are on human scale; there is movement and continuity which provides a series of discoveries, a sense of mystery and magic that is uplifting to the spirit.

This house uplifts my spirit every time I walk in the front door. It is narrow, it occupies almost the entire width of the piece of ground it sits on, which, including half of the driveway, comes to about eighteen feet. It shares its south wall with its Siamese twin next door. Whoever built these pairs of three-storey houses in the late eighteen hundreds must have bought up curlicued iron radiators and stained glass window-panels, moldings and bannisters and wainscotting, in job lots, because almost every house on the street is fitted out just like this one. Sliding doors to left and right off the hall disappear obligingly into the walls, allowing the rooms to open into one another in an agreeably flowing manner. High ceilings give a feeling of airiness and graceful moldings temper harsh angles. In summer the tall windows are wreathed by the rampant ivy sprawling on the brick walls outside that casts a cool green light indoors.

I come downstairs pajama-clad on hot August mornings, walk barefoot through the dining room and across the painted wooden floor of the kitchen, step out into a small paved garden that is enclosed on all sides by an age-darkened cedar fence. It's a garden as private as a room indoors, shaded by trees; a locust and a black walnut tower over the rooftops. Searching tendrils of a wisteria sprawling across the pergola are backlit and illuminated by the rising sun; yellow light falls in long shafts on the brick paving, glints off the water in the scalloped basin of the birdbath and catches the petals of salmon-coloured geraniums in terracotta pots. The resident cardinal announces his dashing presence from a high limb of the walnut tree, drowning out the thin tinnitus of a waking cicada. I don't know whether the elation that fills me means that I've lowered my desires to a point where I am content with little, or that I have learned to extract the happiness contained in each moment with the finesse of a hummingbird taking nectar from a flower. Whichever it is, surges of a larger joy seem to have been supplanted by more frequent, if slighter, glimpses of perfection that I would probably not trade for greater epiphanies even if I could.

The street where I live is a short walk away from the city's first monster house, a structure that would have given Frank Lloyd Wright nightmares. The crenellated stone towers and turrets of Casa Loma are surreal, something left over from a Monty Python movie, but Henry Pellatt, childless businessman and entrepreneur, built the castle as a home for himself and his wife Mary — all ninety-eight rooms, all hundred and eighty thousand square feet of it. Forty servants kept the house and gardens and stables in order. A cathedral-sized pipe organ dominated the great hall; the kitchens were equipped with ovens big enough to accommodate an ox. Sir Henry would probably have found my house only slightly more gracious a place to live in than one of his dog kennels and nowhere near as handsome as the stables where he kept his horses, but then there isn't anything on earth that could have persuaded me to live in his.

Nothing about Casa Loma makes sense. It was never meant to be taken seriously as the Norman-Gothic-Romanesque fortress it pretends to be, and it's just as unbelievable as a private house. It's a marble Venus with a clock in her belly, a chimera, still as inappropriate to its setting in staid Toronto as it was to the early years of the twentieth century when it was built. Form and function hadn't even been properly introduced when it was conceived, let alone wed.

I spent idyllic Saturday evenings at Casa Loma in the forties, dancing cheek to cheek with my high school boyfriend to the big-band music of Ellis McClintock. It was wartime, the swing era, jitterbug days. Notices were posted: *no breaking* — no swinging your partner out to arm's length and whirling her back in again. We danced on the chevron-patterned oak floor of a library fitted with shelves to house ten thousand volumes. Between sets we strolled through massive bronze-and-plate-glass doors into the marble-floored conservatory and drank Cokes under a stained-glass dome backlit by six hundred lights. If the evening was warm the doors in the great hall would be left standing open, so couples could drift out onto the red-tiled terrace and dance dreamily above the city lights, to the strains of *Stardust, String of Pearls, Moonlight Becomes You.*

Those glass and bronze doors leading into the conservatory were copies of a set made in New York for an Italian palazzo and they cost the Pellatts ten thousand dollars each. In those days you could buy an entire house for ten thousand dollars. When I was nine my family moved into an apartment just north of Casa Loma, one of a row of fourplexes built on a portion of the estate Henry had to sell off when his finances began to go sour. The castle was standing cold and empty then, with its lower windows boarded up, and we kids in the neighbourhood made its tangled overgrown gardens our playground, frequently squeezing through a gap in the makeshift fence — put there specifically to keep us out — so we could act out heroic dramas with swords and shields on the very terrace where Sir Henry and Lady Mary had once hosted grand gatherings for troupes of Girl Guides or members of Sir Henry's regiment.

The brick and stone stables with their towers and turrets stood at the end of our street, a few yards from where my family lived. It was rumoured that a long dark tunnel connected the stables to the castle a whole block away (which was true), and we imagined faceless mole-like beings in the dark down there, scurrying back and forth under our feet.

The castle was never finished; creation devoured creator. The Pellatts lived in it for less than ten years before maintenance costs and postwar taxation, along with Sir Henry's bad investments, brought them to financial ruin. The furniture and paintings were sold at auction and the city claimed the castle itself for unpaid taxes. Sir Henry's motto was *Devant Si Je Puis*, and in one way he did lead the pack, if not quite as he intended. The turnout for his funeral was the largest Toronto had ever seen. As for those final ceremonies, let my ashes be quietly cast to fertilize some wooded hillside and the disparate sides of my nature be memorialized with hepaticas and wild garlic.

If I am mildly obsessed with my house the German artist Kurt Schwitters merged with his to the point of total identification. He began to create what was neither sculpture nor architecture but something in between that he called Merzbau, a fantastic construction that grew little by little inside an otherwise quite ordinary small house in Hannover. The project was an escape from the political realities of his time, a private world into which he could withdraw and forget what was happening beyond his doors. He said becoming absorbed in his art was like going to church.

He covered the walls and ceiling in the room he used as a studio with an accumulation of three-dimensional objects and variously shaped structures of wood and paper, cardboard and metal, ceramic, glass, and plaster, and then began to fill the room itself with what he referred to as spoils and relics, a compilation of countless nooks and grottoes which he would then build over and occlude with additions, so that only he knew or could remember what all had gone into it. Before he left Germany and fled to Norway he had "Merzed" eight rooms in his house and his fantastic structure had thrust its way up the shaft to the skylight and through it out onto the roof.

At the centre of Schwitters' Merzbau was a free-standing agglomeration or sculpture that he called The Column of Erotic Misery. Everything of importance to him was represented and contained in it — souvenirs of friends and things of sentimental value were stored in niches and later walled in, among them samples of his own nail parings, hair and urine, and that of his friends. Merzbau was the artist's autobiography, a shrine to his personal reminiscences, his life's work. He began it three times: first in Hannover, a second time in Norway where he fled to escape the Nazis in 1937, and finally, after another flight, in London. Enthusiasts for his work have accorded it a status alongside Abbot Suger's cathedral at St. Denis, but Merzbau lends itself to no classification other than as a work of continuous fluid production, unfinished out of principle. His work, Schwitters said, was an interplay between life and art that was not about the structure itself but about its making, and with that attitude I can't argue. For me the pleasure and satisfaction to be derived from any artistic endeavour — or at least most of it — comes from the process, be it writing a book or painting a picture. Afterward, if the work happens to find an appreciative public, that's just gravy.

The Canadian music critic and writer Eric McLean, my husband's cousin and close friend, lived all his life in Montreal. Eric spent many years and nearly his every penny bringing back into the light of day an eighteenth-century mansion of great elegance in the city's old port, a quarter so tough and down-at-the-heel when he moved into it that it was hazardous to walk its streets after dark. When Eric acquired Maison Papineau in 1967, it was burdened with an ugly two-storey brick addition built above the original roofline, a flophouse for sailors in which the space was cut up into dozens of cubicles just large enough for a bed and a chair. At street level a wholesale fish market and a greasy-spoon restaurant did business, while behind blocked staircases and thrown-up partitions, layers of flooring, false ceilings and peeling wallpaper, boarded-over windows and walls plastered with soft drink advertisements, lay grand and beautifully proportioned rooms, a vast kitchen hearth with its original bake-oven and crane, hand-carved woodwork, splendid tall windows, doors with eighteenth century brass fittings and iron hinges — all cloaked in dross, waiting to be revealed by the artist's chisel — or in this case, his wrecking bar.

While Henry Pellatt's great hall is grandiose, Maison Papineau's noble thirty-foot-long salon is simply — grand. High ceilings meet walls in wide bands of sculpted molding;

tall windows with shutters that fold away on either side are set into deep surrounds. Eric furnished his salon sparingly with an oriental carpet, a grand piano, a few occasional chairs upholstered in faded blue-green velvet. A cushioned sofa faced a pair of wing chairs at either side of the fireplace; a library table held stacks of books and magazines. It was clearly someone's living room, but its function as a place to sit and read the newspaper or practice a fugue on the piano seemed secondary to the room's own intrinsic beauty. In the salon of Maison Papineau I could feel myself expanding in its calm spaciousness and being uplifted by its serenity. Eric sold Maison Papineau to the Canadian Government in 1982, with the proviso that he would live there for the rest of his life, which he did.

I will not be living in this house for the rest of my life. In time, probably sooner than later, three flights of stairs, too many rooms, snow to shovel and a garden to keep will inevitably become too much. I decided that while I was still here I should make some paintings of which the interior of the house would be the subject, and stretched a few canvases in preparation for the project. In one of his more egregiously controversial statements Clement Greenberg said a blank canvas could be considered already existing as a picture, although not necessarily a successful one — to which the critic Michael Fried retorted that a blank canvas might be said to exist as a picture, but *not conceivably as a successful one.* Nevertheless, a new pristine canvas stretched drum-tight and primed with gesso is an attractive object, if one that for the artist is fraught with intimidating expectations. A painting lies hidden within its flat white surface, Art immanent, waiting to be revealed, and, once violated, that flawless plane can no more be restored to oneness than the marble block that's been chiselled away can be put back together again.

When the canvases were ready I walked around the downstairs rooms of my house, sketchbook in hand, making little drawings and working out compositions that could later be expanded into paintings. The dog, curious, followed, flopping down in front of me whenever I paused to choose among various vantage points from which to draw, insinuating herself each time into my interior-scape. I let it happen. The paintings would not be about a dog, but rather paintings that happen to have a dog in them. There are good precedents: Pierre Bonnard, for instance, included his dachshund Ubu in many interior scenes, assigning him no more importance than a teapot. The much larger Sheba may be less easy to accommodate.

I finally settle down on the stair landing, four steps above floor level, with my drawing pad on my knees, and begin to sketch. The three narrow leaded stained glass windows facing me are full of a pink light bouncing off the brick wall of the house on the other side of the mutual driveway to the north; more light is coming from offstage to the left, through the etched glass in the (unseen) front door. There is a curlicued radiator against the wainscotting under the three windows and an old pine table against the wall to the right. The hall floor is made up of black and white tiles; there is a small misshapen nomadic Turkish carpet on the tiles, and on the carpet, the dog.

Those floor tiles have to be dealt with. Squint up the eyes and the black diamonds set into the corners of the larger white squares appear to form rows leading from foreground back to the wainscotted wall, converging toward a vanishing point that might be somewhere in the driveway between this house and the next, or even in *its* front hall. The diamonds appear to get closer together as they recede and become more oblique in shape. Vermeer or Raphael would have plotted and measured and calculated, drawn these squares and diamonds exactly as the eye would see them in real space, but that kind of meticulous attention to perspective verging on *trompe l'oeil* is no longer necessary or desirable. I go for a looser solution in my drawing and arrange them by eye, reducing them in number to cramp spatial depth as they progress toward their vanishing point. If the floor doesn't look flat enough to walk on and the space appears shallower than it actually is, I will not be troubled. What I will be creating (*pace* Clement Greenberg) is not a floor but a design on a two-dimensional surface.

The pine table with its blue-painted legs and apron must agree with the perspective of the floor, or it will look crippled. The three windows cast light on the table's top and turn it pink in places; the reflections of its legs in the gloss of the floor dive below the surface to float down and meet the carpet. Some of those black diamond-shaped tiles pick up a film of blue or gray or pink light and don't look black anymore. In shadow the white tiles have a violet cast, and there's a touch of yellowish green in them from that unseen window to the left. I make colour notes about what I see, but in the end I'm the one in charge, and if the colours I need for my effects aren't the ones I'm noting at the side of my drawing I will choose others for the sake of the painting.

The large tiles and the wainscotting and wall and radiator are white in real life, but on my canvas I will use no white paint other than as a bright spot or two on the glazed surface of a lamp that sits on the table and in the stained glass windows. If I were to squander my brightest pigment I would have nothing left for highlights, so all those white surfaces will have to be expressed in nacreous violets, blues, grays and pinks, ochres and buffs. The dog is black and tan, camouflage gear that blends in with the russet and blackish colours of the patterned carpet on which she lies, and if I am skilful enough I will make her almost disappear, big as she is and occupying so much of the foreground. Find the dog in this picture. Up in my studio I take a thin stick of charcoal and start breaching the integrity of one of those pristine white canvases, reproducing with light strokes an enlarged version of the drawing I made from my vantage point on the landing. Slowly, as the days go by, I will build up the surface of the painting with hundreds of short brush strokes, hoping that when it is finished it will convey something of my deep sense of connectedness with this house, and the way its various elements seem to unfold toward me and begin demanding my attention when I come downstairs in the morning.

Solstices

On the exact morning of the vernal equinox, with an uncalculated precision that would have made the builders of Stonehenge grind their teeth in envy, the sun sends a fireball directly through the east-facing window of my attic aerie, smiting the screen of my computer with an explosion of light that makes what I'm trying to write unreadable. My response to that marking of the new season is as casual as was my earlier decision about where I would set up the computer. I cover the windowpane with a small plastic tablecloth salvaged from the detritus of some bygone summer, hitch it with the help of a yardstick onto hooks screwed for the purpose into the top of the window frame, and leave it there for a few weeks until the sun has moved on. In autumn, when the sun has wheeled up to its zenith, gone into reverse and returned to the same point on its way south for the winter, my makeshift blind goes up again.

At the June solstice I perform another unremarkable but necessary sun-ceremony. The street where I live appears to lie on a north-south line, but it actually angles from southeast to northwest, as do many such streets in this city due to their arising at right angles to the slanted shoreline of Lake Ontario. Because of this purely subjective disorientation, each June the sun reaches a position in the late afternoon sky which appears to be north of the house rather than due west where it belongs, a matter of no consequence were it not that again, when I am at my computer, a blinding ray pierces a skylight set in the north slope of the roof, which in theory ought not to admit afternoon sun at all. I then rig a light-diffusing cover for the skylight, an invention of my own consisting of a folded sheet of newspaper, trimmed and laid neatly between the glass of the skylight and its fitted screen, and leave it in place until the sun vacates that piece of sky for another year, or when tiny brown fragments of toasted newspaper begin sifting through the screen into my hair.

In the small garden behind this narrow inner-city house, notice that fall has arrived comes in the form of a dangerous hail of nuts clad in spiky green jackets, each the size and weight of a golfball. They come pelting out of the black walnut tree in the yard next door, striking a metal garage roof with gunshot reports and catapulting into our garden where they roll around on the flagstones, or, if they've smacked themselves directly into a flower bed, come to rest half-buried in the soil, like meteors landing in a desert.

As the sun sinks lower, a shadow is cast by the six-foot cedar fence that separates our property from that of our neighbours to the south where the walnut tree is, a shadow at first a mere foot or so wide, then several feet, then a few yards, then half the garden, until by December, when the sun's daily rising and setting has become almost perfunctory, all but a few feet of the narrow garden lies

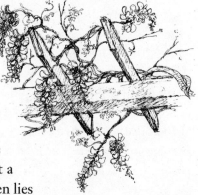

in the shade of the cedar fence. I then begin to watch that shadow recede as winter drags along with maddening slowness, noting the line of demarcation between sun and shade as it creeps southward across the snow, comparing it with where it was the week before, noticing with excitement that the sun is almost on the bird bath, that it's taken in the bird bath and is hitting the top of the lilac bush, that now it's lighting up the tendrils of wisteria that twist dryly on the pergola. Even in the last half of April, when the rest of the garden has thawed and bulbs are up and ready to flower and the forsythia is in bloom, the shadowed earth at the base of the fence remains cold and hard, a small subarctic microclimate in which the few tough ferns and wild violets that survive there emerge reluctantly from the chill wet ground.

One mid-January day, while I was eating breakfast and staring bleakly out at the almost entirely shadowed garden, the weatherman on the radio remarked that the sun had come up that morning in Cambridge Bay for the first time since the middle of November. Counting my blessings, I looked up Cambridge Bay in an atlas and then in the encylopedia and learned that the settlement's proper name is Iqaluktuutiaq; that it is situated in an area of sags and swells, dry debris-strewn knolls and moist depressions with very little vegetation, on Victoria Island, in Nunavut, Canada's third territory which comprises one-fifth — *one-fifth!* — of this vast country in which I was born and have spent most of my life. The map in my atlas shows Victoria Island more or less beside Baffin Island and south of Ellesmere Island, and after Ellesmere there's nothing but sea and ice all the way to the North Pole. From the encyclopedia I read, among other pertinent facts about the area's topography, that a visual reminder of early Arctic exploration, the hull of Roald Amundsen's vessel the *Maud*, sticks up out of the water of the bay in summer and through the ice in winter, within view of the town.

I have never travelled to the Arctic, but my imagination often roams to my country's vast *beyond* — over the bony precambrian shield, the scattered lakes with pine-clad rocky shores, thinning scrub gradually dwindling to featureless tundra, lichen-spattered rock, sea ice. I've noticed that on US television stations all weather comes to an abrupt halt at the Canadian border, beyond which no temperatures are posted and everything is coloured icy blue, as though the whole country were a vast refrigerator too cold to support life. I suppose all of Canada, from the middle of the Great Lakes to the North Pole, is the *beyond* for our neighbours to the south. The fact that Toronto lies at a more southerly latitude than the northern tip of California — a thought that has always given me comfort — apparently doesn't cut any ice.

As a child I was taught that Toronto was fortunate in being situated in a temperate zone — not too hot, not too cold, just right. I was shown pictures of the people then called Eskimos, who lived in igloos and travelled over the frozen wastes by dogsled. My mind could accept that there was a part of the country where it was winter almost all year round and children sucked on hollow bird's legs filled with blubber instead of lollypops, but I was not convinced of the reverse, the existence of places that were always hot. The swaying palm trees and dazzling beaches in Carmen Miranda's wartime movies were to me on the same level of fantasy as Carmen's banana-and-pineapple headdresses and the way a troupe of dancers and an eight-piece mariachi band would appear out of nowhere every time she got the urge to dance and break into song. People in my family's circumstances didn't travel far from home during the thirties, not at all during the forties when the war was on and gas was rationed, nor in the unsettled years that immediately followed. Until I lived for a time in England, where spring arrives just as winter is beginning to get under way, I took it for granted that the seasons everwhere were pretty much like our own.

On a TV programme I happened to catch one day, the English actor Michael Caine spoke about his difficulty in adjusting to the benevolence of the southern California climate after the damp cool of London. When he bought some plants for his new home in Los Angeles he asked the nurseryman when he could set them out. The man looked at him as though he were soft in the head. "When you get home," he said.

We here in southern Ontario must be more careful with our setting out. The date after which "all danger of frost has passed," as it says on the seed packets, has traditionally been the twenty-fourth of May, although there are always a few risk-takers hoping to get a head start by planting annuals a week or two earlier. Gardeners are forever pushing the limits of endurance of growing things. When I lived in Calgary during the sixties I planted forsythia bushes, without whose yellow flowers I felt spring simply wouldn't be spring. I grieved when the few that survived the long hard winters failed to flower, all the while looking with scorn on the ubiquitous caragana shrubs growing everywhere that were nonchalantly putting out an abundance of perfectly good yellow blooms spring after spring.

Maybe it's perverse, trying to persuade plants to endure climates they never would have chosen for themselves. I coddle a wisteria vine in my Toronto garden, a first cousin to the Calgary caragana and one of the huge family of Fabaceae, of which there are some ten thousand species scattered across the earth including all the vetches and peas and beans, the lupins and clovers. The individual flowers of the wisteria are almost identical to those of the Calgary caraganas and also to the multitudes of white flowers that come sifting down from the tremendously tall acacia tree that towers between our Toronto garden and that of our neighbours. The acacia is a fine nesting place for crows but it scarcely merits a glance from any of us whether it's in bloom or not. The acacia, or "pseudoacacia" as my tree book insists, can withstand neglect and heat and drought, it's pest-free and disease resistant; it produces masses of fragrant white flowers every spring and at the end of each summer day its tall feathery canopy is the last thing touched by the sun's rays.

I don't understand my own unwillingness to accept what nature and the climate offer, why I ignore my very own towering pseudoacacia tree and cultivate a wisteria that required a large wooden pergola to be constructed at considerable expense for its especial comfort and happiness. It would much rather be in Sicily or the south of France or even damp old England, in any of which places it would grow a trunk as thick as a footballer's leg and sprawl and bloom abundantly. In Toronto's climate wisteria takes years of development before it will consider blooming, requires more sunlight than my inner-city garden can easily provide and needs careful pruning if it is to be kept from shooting off in all directions and failing to flower at all — in short, it's a pain in the neck. If the spring is cold the wisteria blooms late and in the blast of early summer heat its heavy bunches of mauve flowers last only a few days. All this, so that for one brief week my garden can be a pseudoGiverney.

Up in Iqaluktuutiaq, where the sun appeared on that mid-January day after two months of darkness, the landscape is sparsely dotted with the small stone structures called Inuksuit which the Innuit build, they say, to act in the capacity of a human. They are set up on the bleak terrain by subsequent generations of travellers to mark places where hunting and fishing is particularly good, to create sight lines and warn of dangers or to indicate good routes to follow — or even just to say, "I was here."

Occasionally, in the shelter of one of them, a plant that has no business being there at all manages to flourish in a bit of gritty soil that is protected from the icy winds and warmed by the sun. Lichens crumble and fall to enrich it; birds perch on the Inuksuit and leave droppings and undigested seeds. After a while the seeds germinate and tiny Arctic plants appear and bloom. When I read about this phenomenon I decided that if such delicate vegetation can show so much heroic adaptability and endurance my wisteria should consider itself lucky to be in the much more sympathetic climate of southern Ontario.

This year, the day the plastic tablecloth went up, I stepped out the door of my writing room onto the small wooden deck that sits on the flat roof of the second-storey bedroom below. The deck is surrounded by a solid five-foot-high cedar railing, so it is like a cup held up to the sky, trapping the sun and keeping the wind at bay. There was still snow on the ground down below and no sign of green on the trees, but at noon that March day it was so warm up there that I was able to stretch out on a plastic chaise longue in shirt sleeves, close my eyes, and risk all by turning my pale face up to the ruinous rays of the sun. My two cats, both in their thirteenth year, followed me outdoors and sprawled on the warm gray wooden boards of the deck with their furry bellies exposed gratefully to the heat.

With my closed eyes protected by sunglasses, I let my ears take over and began sorting out the sounds that came drifting in on the mild air. The hum of traffic on nearby busy streets was continuous, punctuated by the odd blast of a car horn. From a few doors to the north, where a pair of three-storey

Victorian houses was being converted to six condos, came sounds of hammering and sawing; the workmen shouted to each other over the rap music blaring out of their radio. From below, down in the garden, came the chatter of birds squabbling around the feeder I hang from the pergola through winter and early spring. I could distinguish the warbling and trilling of house finches, the small sparrow-sized gray-brown birds that look as though they'd been dipped head first into raspberry juice. They don't really belong here. In 1940 a number of pet shop owners on Long Island were forced by law to release the dozens of illegally caged house finches that had been trapped and brought east from their native California, and from Long Island the finches spread south and westward until they met the indigenous populations from the west coast. But some came north as far as southern Ontario, where they were quckly obliged to teach themselves the whole new behaviour of migrating south for the winter and returning in the spring — another example of the admirable adaptability of living things. But what baffles me is why they come back. Multitudes of Canadians prefer to lock up their houses and spend the winters in condos and trailer parks in Florida than stay up here in the blue belt, but unlike human migrants those finches don't own real estate that pulls them back to their northern homes.

On that March morning the house finches had returned in large numbers and so had the so-called robins that are not genuine robins at all but a red-breasted native thrush, as well as several varieties of woodpecker and the grackles with their burnished plumage. The grackle's song, if it can be called that, is described in the bird books as resembling the squeal of a rusty gate, but to me it is a sound from the Monday mornings of my childhood, the repeated short screeches of wire clothesline being hauled around the pulley-wheels rigged from everybody's back stoop to a handy tree or a pole at the end of the yard. Through the general cacophony I could distinguish the more euphonious *scree scree* of a couple of red-winged blackbirds that had dropped by to stoke up at the feeder before heading off to the ponds in the old brickworks park. A few Canada geese flew overhead, honking, birds that gave up migrating many goose-generations ago to raise their young in Toronto's parks in the spring and then spend the rest of the year hanging around the waterfront making nuisances of themselves. Their less urbane cousins would be along a little later, flying much higher through April skies in long lovely skeins, heading for their breeding grounds on Victoria and Baffin Islands.

What were subsequent generations of those immigrant Long Island house finches thinking of when they found they had to fly south every year to survive the winters, and then make the long journey back? Why, when they realized that the magical midnight twilights of Iqaluktuutiaq always gave way to months of perpetual darkness, did the ancestors of the present-day Innuit stay on and make the icy attics of the world their permanent homes? Why not pack up and follow the sun across the water to the mainland, travel southward down the shores of Hudson Bay and overland to Lake Ontario where the climate is temperate — not too hot, not too cold — and the sun shines every month of the year? Why, I ask myself, did my paternal great-grandfather, a carpenter and builder who came here from England in the mid-eighteen hundreds, build a house for himself and his family on the side of the canal in Campbellford, Ontario? He'd travelled this far, why not carry on southward to the lowlands of South Carolina, say, where winter is brief and snow is rarely even seen, or farther, to Mississippi or Louisiana, where it's warm even in midwinter? Was it that things somehow looked right to him in Campbellford? When it comes to that, why have I lived up here in the blue belt for three quarters of a century?

It must be that this place has had a larger part than I realized in the making of me, the forming of whatever or whoever it is I am. My nature has been shaped by its four strongly marked and actually quite immoderate seasons. I would miss watching their passing and anticipating their coming — the months of frost and snow, the chill reluctant springs, sweltering summers that leave us gasping, and brilliant autumns that can transform themselves practically overnight into bleak bare-branched Novembers.

I stepped off an airplane in Barbados once, feeling my winter-shrivelled self expanding in air so palpably moist and healing that I wanted to gather handfuls of it and rub it into my skin. While blizzards raged in Toronto I lay in hot pink bliss on a white beach and refreshed myself in the bath-warm blue-green sea. Nevertheless, after two weeks I was ready to go home. I felt out of place in the tropics, the way a penguin in the San Diego zoo must feel. The rattling palms were not my trees; I didn't know the names of the birds that sang in the mornings or what species of creature it was that shrilled in the shrubbery at night. The extravagant flowers blooming everywhere looked artificial and flamboyant to my eyes. Endless summer would be no more my cup of tea than the perpetual Arctic winter.

From the hotel terrace in Barbados I observed descendants of the mongooses that were brought to the island from India to kill the rats in the sugar cane (which they failed to do) darting in and out of the hedges of the hotel garden, their bellies so close to the ground they looked as though they were on wheels. Interesting and funny creatures, but when it comes to feeling kinship with wild animals, I'll take the brazen young raccoon that for the past week has been enjoying the warmth of my third-floor deck and glares at me with bright-eyed indignation whenever I step out to luxuriate in what he has come to consider his personal patch of spring sun.

Second Sight

Plato was probably right when he said that the root of artistic creation was an inspired madness. Artists can be obsessives, driven human beings who can't entertain the thought of quitting even when they're overtaken by old age and infirmity. During his last years Renoir painted with his brushes strapped to hands gnarled with arthritis; aged and half-blind Monet combined his pigments from memory while he painted one of the major masterpieces of his life. Bonnard lay on his deathbed giving directions to his niece, who was looking after him, precisely where she was to dab a few more brush-loads of colour on what turned out to be his final painting. But it's not only geniuses who are obsessed. As a non-genius painter even I can't imagine still being on this earth and not wanting to draw and paint. Maybe the way to bring on real craziness is to prevent an artist from working.

Art was never Plato's favourite thing anyway. In his view anything from the natural world, a pot of geraniums, let us say, is sandwiched between an immaterial Ideal Form of geraniums — of which the plant itself is already an imitation — and the final imitation that is the artist's image. To him art was at worst a dangerous delusion and at best an entertainment. Here Plato and I part company. I think an artist's goal and what fuels his or her desire is neither to translate into material form some abstract concept of Beauty, nor to make a lifelike copy of that wretched pot of geraniums, but something else entirely. I have never begun a painting or even a drawing without first having had not only a fleeting vision in my mind's eye of how

the finished work will (or should) look but what kind of emotion it will arouse in me when I see it, and that moment of intuition is not only what sets me going but is the standard by
which I will judge the piece at the end. While there is the rare
euphoria-inducing occasion when it seems almost impossible
to make a wrong brush stroke, most of the time I only come
close to where I want to go and frequently fail altogether. The
thing may be well enough executed but it will have a kind of
slackness, a lack of energy and compression, so that the feeling
is weakly expressed or missing altogether. The strange part is
that far from discouraging me, my failures egg me on to start
anew and this time get it right, and around I go again.

Where the fleeting vision comes from that stamps itself
so firmly on my mind's eye is a mystery, but what is certain is
that it calls the shots, and if the phenomenon is as universal
as I believe it to be, it shows no more mercy toward the genius
than to the artist of small talent. Cézanne wrestled through
more than a hundred sittings for which the dealer Ambroise
Vollard patiently posed before the artist finally abandoned the
project, remarking, as he tossed down his brush and shoved the
canvas into a corner, that he was not entirely displeased with
the shirt-front. No one but Cézanne himself could know what
he found unsatisfactory about that never-finished painting.

Not that eyesight of the ordinary kind doesn't affect an artist's
work. I have read that the figures in El Greco's monumental
works may have been so strangely elongated because he had
astigmatism, and that Monet probably used so much blue in
his later paintings because that was one of the few colours he
could still see. From my own recent experience I've begun to
wonder if Claude Lorraine had cataracts and painted all his
romantic Italian landscapes bathed in a golden-umber light
because that was the way he saw them.

For my part I prefer blue Italian skies to look blue, or rather that colour into which our eyes translate empty space, but over a period of two or three years I became aware that an ochre-coloured cloud was dulling the colour of my own Canadian skies, darkening the page I was reading, smudging my drawings and fogging the words on my computer-screen. The cataracts were at first a nuisance and then a trial and finally an intolerable despoiler of everything my eyes fell upon. The ophthalmologist I consulted showed me a little bottle of formaldehyde containing the cataracted lens from a human eye. It looked like a bead of tapioca dipped in coffee or dabbed with yellow-brown paint. No wonder my view of the world was jaundiced. I decided to go ahead and have the surgery he recommended, even though the thought of letting someone go at my eyes with a knife was, to say the least, daunting.

I arrived at the hospital early in the morning during the tail-end of Toronto's outbreak of Severe Acute Respiratory Syndrome. Did I have fever, chills, a cough or difficulty breathing? No. Was anyone in my family ill? No. Had I visited another health-care facility during the past two weeks? No. I was handed a mask and told to clean my hands with antiseptic gel.

Upstairs in the day-surgery department I was shown to a cubicle, told to take everything off and put on two cotton hospital gowns, one forward and one backward, plus plastic shower cap, paper shoes, and another mask. A plastic ID bracelet was fastened to my wrist. In a waiting area I was assigned a comfortable Archie Bunker chair with extending footrest and a kindly person wrapped a warmed flannelette sheet around me. Two other capped and masked patients tucked up in their own chairs had been watching me settle in; we smiled at one another by crinkling our eyes.

That I was nervous as a cat showed in my elevated blood pressure when they took it. Today's surgery would be on my right eye and several kinds of drops were now put in it, of which some stung mightily. A needle with a syringe tube attached was inserted into a vein in the back of my hand, capped off and taped down. In due time an orderly came to lead me and the two other patients, all of us trailing our blankies, down a corridor, onto an elevator, off again on a higher floor and through a pair of doors marked DO NOT ENTER, at which point he was relieved of his charges and we were shown to another waiting area.

A nurse carrying a clipboard sat down beside each of us in turn, checking things off. Was this my signature giving consent to the operation? I was without my glasses, so I couldn't actually read anything because of the rotten vision in one eye and the other being completely out of it from the drops, but I said yes. Was I allergic to anything, did I have diabetes, could I climb a flight of stairs, could I — not *would* I but *could* I — tell her my date of birth? Yes I could: six six twenty-seven I said smartly. She checked that off, stood up, took my arm and led me through another set of doors into a brilliantly lit room where a group of masked and gowned people were standing around a white-sheeted table. Among them I recognized my eye doctor, who greeted me and helped me onto the table.

I lay there with nothing to do while they fussed around with equipment. They stuck some leads on me here and there and I noticed with bemused interest that a rhythmic beeping from somewhere behind my head was cleverly coinciding with the beating of my heart. Now a spurt of cold liquid shot up my forearm through the needle in the back of my hand and seconds later I felt a spreading warmth, like the first good swallow of a straight-up extra-dry martini. Now they were rolling the lid of my right eye up on a handy matchstick so I couldn't close it any more — but no matter, someone began sluicing the eye comfortingly with tepid water.

I sighed deeply, without moving of course, just to let them know I was still in there. Suddenly a dark tunnel appeared in my field of vision, and at the end of it, a dazzling white light. If I was being launched on that final journey through space and time to where Glory awaits, I thought, I'd better pay close attention in case I wanted to describe it later to some old friend in the next world. There was a little intermittent whirring noise, like a dentist's drill with the sound turned away down. Kaleidoscopic colours and lights appeared, sparkled and fragmented and reassembled. More whirring. More lights, more colours, some red, some blue, some a blurry mixture. No pain, no pressure, just a sense that things were going on close to where I lived.

I had a pretty good idea of what was happening because I'd read up on it ahead of time. The doctor had made a tiny incision in my eye where the coloured part meets the white, through which he inserted an ultrasound-tipped probe to break apart the cataract and then vacuum out the pieces, leaving behind the little cup called a posterior capsule in which the natural lens used to sit. In the olden days surgery had to wait until the cataract had matured, or ripened, as they called it, which really meant hardened to the point that it could be plucked out like a dried pea. In the days before the invention of modern suturing materials the eye had to heal on its own, while the patient lay abed with his head sandbagged down to keep him from shifting around and disrupting the healing process. Sutures were used later, but even then, with no lens in his eye to focus light onto the retina, the patient would have to wear bottle-bottom glasses for the rest of his life. Nowadays implanted lenses are made-to-measure for the customer from space-age plastics, and the incision is shaped in such a way that the fluid pressure inside the eye miraculously seals it shut without the need for any sutures at all.

When it was over a nurse helped me to sit up on the edge of the table, and I perched there for a moment, collecting myself. She stood in front of me, steadying me with a gentle hand on my shoulder, and to my freshly hatched eye, even with its enormously dilated pupil and overflow of fogging tears, her gown was the most astonishing blue I had ever seen, a blue so remarkable that I closed the new eye and looked at this phenomenon with my other, unoperated-upon eye. There was the blue I'd become accustomed to over the years, a dulled down greenish-brownish melancholy blue with all the power drained out of it, the blues of the Sistine Chapel ceiling before the layers of varnish and dirt were cleaned away.

Back home, still drowsy, I flopped down on the sofa between the windows in the dining room. My glance fell on a blue pitcher on the serving table across the room, a kitchen item really, but its shape was appealing so I kept it in view and used it occasionally as a vase for flowers. I stared. What was it with blue? Like that nurse's gown, the pitcher was so blue I could have wept for its blueness, I could have dived into that blue and submerged myself in it, been absorbed by it. It was cerulean sort  of hue but with a little more purple to it, maybe a touch of cobalt or ultramarine but not enough to make it dark or turn it into the kind of blue that backs away and lets other colours take precedence. This blue was right here, *present*, on the surface of the air, like the blues in one of Bonnard's paintings of the descending terraces at Le Cannet, with their red roofs and palms and pines and finally the distant azure sea, and above it all a great arc of the infinite Mediterranean sky. His last canvas, painted at the age of eighty, was of an almond tree in bloom against just such a sky, just such a blue.

Monet was seventy-two when he was diagnosed with cataracts in both eyes. He was offered surgery, beginning with the eye most seriously afflicted, but was afraid to undergo it in case he lost his sight in the eye entirely. I could sympathize. Even as I walked into the operating room I wondered if some unexpected anomaly would crop up and I'd end up worse off than I was before. I could still see, after all, even if what I saw was blurred and tarnished. When Monet faced his decision in nineteen-twelve there were no antibiotics to prevent or combat infection, no steroid drops to reduce swelling, no cunning stitchless self-closing incisions, no lasers, no ultrasound probes. He turned it down.

Eleven years later his vision had degenerated to the point that it was virtually non-existent in the right eye and there was only ten percent remaining in the left. With so little sight in that right eye he figured he had nothing to lose. He entered the clinic in Neuilly and underwent surgery, after which the eye was kept bandaged for ten days and another twenty days passed before he was fitted with corrective glasses. As it turned out the surgery helped with his close vision but the distance vision remained far from good, and colours were elusive. Later, when a celebrated ophthalmologist visited him at Giverny and asked how his eyes were coming along Monet said, "Je vois bleu, mais je ne vois plus le rouge, je ne vois plus le jaune."

Now, in order to paint with colours he could no longer see, he chose them by their names on the tubes, mixing the pigments in the proportions he knew would produce the oranges and greens and violets, the rosy hues and the russets and golds of his garden. Some art historians, determined to look on the bright side, like to claim that his diminished sight opened up new spheres for him, a more inward vision that was dependent on knowledge and spiritual insight rather than direct perception. What is true is that he knew the colours of his garden at Giverny in a way that he could not have known those of any other landscape, since he himself had designed and supervised the construction of every path and bridge, planned the ponds, laid out the shapes of the flower beds and directed the planting of all that was to grow therein. He worked in a hangar-like studio in a corner of his garden, choosing colours and forms dictated by his mind's eye while he painted the series for which he has become most famous, the enormous water-lily panels that were later installed according to his own directions in the Orangerie in Paris.

Monet once said he wasn't sure deep down whether he was actually more a gardener or a painter. Marcel Proust, who was an avid admirer of Monet's work, said that if one day he could see M. Claude Monet's garden he felt sure he would be looking at something that was not so much a natural flower garden as a colour garden, because it was planted in such a way that only the flowers with matching colours would bloom at the same time, harmonized in an infinite stretch of blue or pink. In those latter years the artist would have been able to see only the broad forms of his ponds and willow trees and bridges and of the details not much at all, but it seems not to have mattered. The artist, after all, strives not to imitate nature but to imitate its Creator, and art needs no reality beyond its own. As Proust said, "Le peintre traverse le miroir magique de la réalité."

I checked around the dining room. With my new eye the yellow wallpaper appeared to be brighter, clearer, but not altogether changed in character the way the blue was. The same for the coral-red seats of the chairs, which looked as though

they'd had a good washing perhaps, but were not utterly different. It seemed that although blue had been forced to reveal
itself in previously unimagined brilliance, red and yellow were
still more or less able to take my new powers in stride. It had
been a dull and rainy morning, but after my belated breakfast
I noticed that the sun was coming out, so I walked into the living room and looked toward the large front window. In the
sudden blast of light tears sprang and flooded my new and still
photophobic eye, but through the mist I could see the fresh
rosy brick of the house across the street, the sparkle of a bicycle anchored to its iron railings, the deep viridian leaves of
the maple tree next door, the dazzling emerald of the vines
around the windows. And the sky. Oh my God, the blue sky!

The Real Thing

During the early seventies I was renting studio space in a warehouse with three other artists, one of whom was projecting transparencies of well-known masterpieces directly onto stretched canvases and copying them in oils, right down to simulating age-cracks in the paint with a fine brush. Artists were still listening to Clement Greenberg and the flatness-Nazis back then, and I wondered if my studio-mate had found his way around them by choosing as his subjects these images which were themselves unarguably two-dimensional, but which gave him the freedom to paint in an illusory third dimension. Not so, it seemed. He told me his work was conceptual. The point was that the art-object should cease to be an end in itself and become no more than the idea from which it had sprung, which is the essence of a work of art. His paintings, he explained, were not copies, but reinterpretations, an analysis of the original concepts of those famous artists by which he was generating a new idea — the comparison of his copies with the originals — and so in conceptual terms, they themselves were original art.

He said all this with blue-eyed straight-faced sincerity, and I thought if he believed in what he was saying, it was irony beyond irony. He had stumbled through the looking glass into a postmodern virtual world in which value judgements and concepts like truth and beauty were declared meaningless, only to make the judgement that his own declarations were both significant and true. As far as I was concerned his belaboured copies were neither art nor an interpretation of art, and the notion that the idea behind a painting could supplant the work itself is as ludicrous as saying the recipe could take the place of the ragout. His copies clearly did not spring from an internal creative compulsion, and despite his justifying arguments and the measure of critical acclaim his work may eventually have received, the likely truth was that he lacked visual imagination and probably couldn't draw. There may be those who would call such work a postmodern celebration of meaninglessness, but like the kid in the New Yorker cartoon, I say it's spinach, and I say to hell with it. If the real world fails to live up to the artist's expectations he is free to reinvent it according to his own subjective insights, which is not a matter of argument, but of art.

Every journal and magazine I opened in those days seemed to feature an article by some high-powered New York critic announcing that easel painting, which had been seriously ill for a long time, was now officially dead. I was then just returning to painting after a long hiatus, and I felt like shouting *just a damned minute.* The winds of postmodernism were beginning to sweep through the galleries and museums, driving out the pictures and leaving in their wake installations of building materials, amateurish videos, printed polemics and things floating in glass jars, while drawing, the most poetic of all art forms, was being replaced by photography. If easel painting was dead, my heart was in the coffin there with Cézanne.

Borrowing images or compositions from other artists — or quoting from them, as it's sometimes called — is a legitimate enough practice. Michelangelo, Cellini, Rubens, Rembrandt, Fragonard, Delacroix, Degas, Manet — all were unabashed quoters. An artist is free to make use of whatever he can find that will help give form to what is in his mind's eye, whether he quotes from the work of another artist or uses mechanical devices that get him where he wants to go. All art-making is a mechanical process at some level, and it wasn't my studio-mate's use of slides and a projector I found fault with but his limp theories and the paint-by-numbers results he thought should be given serious consideration. An artist of inspired imagination can metamorphose a technical process into a work of art, as David Hockney did when he set aside his painting and drawing tools for a while to make a series of stunning collages out of dozens of polaroid snapshots. Even Leonardo might have tried out polaroids or slides and a projector if he could have laid hands on them. As it was he called the mirror the master and guide of painters because it displays a three-dimensional subject on a flat surface just the way a painting does, and he raved about the camera obscura, which is in effect a room-sized pinhole camera. "Who would believe that so small a space could contain the image of all the universe?" he wrote in his notebooks. "O mighty process!"

Hockney makes a convincing case in his recent book, *Secret Knowlege: Rediscovering the Lost Techniques of the Old Masters*, as to how artists such as Holbein and Vermeer and Caravaggio began to achieve such strikingly accurate perspective and meticulous detail in their paintings and suddenly were able to foreshorten horribly difficult things like musical instruments and human hands — all too fine and perfect, Hockney says, to have been accomplished by mere "eyeballing." He believes they used the camera obscura and the camera lucida, along with lenses and prisms and mirrors that acted as overhead projectors, reflecting images of living subjects or still-life set-ups directly onto their canvases. The camera obscura turns images not only upside down but transposes them laterally, left to right, and Hockney bolsters his argument by pointing out the spate of left-handed figures that began to appear at a time when left-handedness was still considered — well — sinister. Vermeer didn't leave any written notes as to how he achieved his miraculous results, so no one knows whether Hockney is right, but then as he says, few really care how Vermeer created his masterpieces, least of all Hockney himself.

Borrowing is one thing, but appropriating an image, making alterations to it and then claiming it as an original is something else again. In the hushed and perfumed lounge of the spa in an upmarket Toronto hotel there hangs an unlovely parody of a 1935 painting by Pierre Bonnard, one of several studies he made of his wife soaking herself in the bathtub. The plagiarizer has stuck some criss-crossed strips of what looks like gauze bandage into the paint as a substitute for Bonnard's luscious rendering of the tiles on the floor and behind the tub — no doubt because reproducing those nacreous tones was beyond the man's capabilities — but the composition, the oddly shaped old-fashioned bathtub and the nude figure of Marthe lying in it have been copied straight from the original. The soi-disant artist even had the chutzpah to sign his own name to this abortion. He must have been the interior decorator's out-of-work cousin.

That horrible daub on the wall of the spa aroused my ire to such a degree that it all but ruined the pleasure of the pedicure I had come for in the first place. Pierre Bonnard is, hands down, my favourite artist of all time. Why that should be I can't fully explain because the emotional response to works· of art can't easily be expressed in words, but I believe it's at least in part because of the passionate tenderness with which Bonnard observes ordinary scenes of domestic life. His paintings of these subjects — luncheon on a terrace in the south of France, a woman pouring tea or feeding her dog tidbits at the table, his garden, his lifelong companion and model Marthe at her toilette — all seem to say that this is all we need, ever, for art and for life. There may have been a dark side to his nature, as some of his self-portraits would suggest, but even that darkness, where it appears, is expressed as a kind of ecstasy.

When, during the first flaming of my love affair with Bonnard's work, I looked up his dates and discovered that I had shared this planet with him during the last twenty years of his life and the first twenty of mine, I was suffused with a strange joy.

My outrage at the plagiarized version of Bonnard's work had partly to do with the desecration of a lovely image about which I felt almost possessive, and partly with something else that is not easy for me to admit. When you admire the work of a particular artist to the degree that I admire Bonnard's, it requires tremendous restraint and vigilance to absorb his influence without half-unconsciously imitating the colours and subjects and mood of his work, since those are the very elements you love. This inner battle of mine is compounded by the fact that when I do paint something that satisfies me, I am never quite certain whether I am pleased with it because it expresses something from my own inner self or because it vibrates to some small degree with a certain Bonnard-ness. It's a dilemma I may never be able to resolve.

A problem more universal than being entranced with a particular artist's work is the danger of gradually starting to imitate oneself, falling into the trap of repeating what has been satisfying or successful in the past rather than taking chances and letting the work develop organically — which is not at all a matter of changing one's preferred motifs but of developing a more profound perception of them. The problem is reflexive and one that the public is unlikely to care about it, or even take notice of, when it begins to occur. If an artist gets into a stylistic rut he may find that his public will happily absorb any number of virtually interchangeable snowbound Quebec villages or bleak Georgian Bay shores, and decide, to the satisfaction of his dealer and his fans and even himself, that he will stay with what works.

Forging an exact copy of an existing work (preferably not one on display in the Louvre) or creating a new work that counterfeits the style of a well-known artist and passing it off as the real thing, is something else again. With new technologies, faking art prints would probably be a piece of cake, but then prints don't bring in high returns considering the risks involved in marketing them; if you're making funny money you don't print one-dollar bills. Manufacturing a pseudo-Hockney painting would be a good investment of time, but the real money has always lain in creating and then pretending to bring to light works by famous artists of bygone eras, a much more difficult undertaking considering that the materials must pass muster as well as the images, but hugely rewarding if it can be gotten away with.

Just after the end of the second world war the Canadian newspapers were full of the story of a Dutch art dealer named Han van Meegeren. During the German occupation van Meegeren had sold a Vermeer to Hermann Goering, commander-in-chief of the Luftwaffe and president of the Reichstag, who had gleefully carted his treasure back to his home in Berlin. The painting was never seen again but the transaction itself had not gone unnoticed. When the war was over van Meegeren was charged with collaboration and selling off national treasures, but after a few weeks in prison he confessed that the painting had been a forgery of his own making, and what's more he'd faked several other Vermeers and a couple of Pieter de Hooghs as well. When the forger was asked by the courts to prove the painting he'd sold to Goering was a fake, he had materials brought to the prison and painted a new Vermeer right before their eyes. The charges of collaboration were dropped, and although the man had become something of a national hero for pulling a fast one on Goering, he was then charged with forgery.

Canadians were feeling special kinship with the Dutch at that time. Members of the Dutch royal family had spent the war years in Ottawa as guests of the Canadian Government, and when Crown Princess Juliana gave birth to a child in an Ottawa hospital room it was temporarily declared Dutch territory so the royal infant wouldn't be born on foreign soil. I was studying at the University of Toronto when the Van Meegeren story broke, and it was introduced as the subject of a fine art seminar. The unsympathetic Dutch press had described him as the "Dutch Nazi artist," but in the American newspapers and a lengthy *Saturday Evening Post* article he was glorified as heroic, an anti-Nazi Dutch hero who had cheated Hermann Goering. We students took the more lenient view. Van Meegeren had been a frustrated genius, our little group decided, trying to scratch together a living for his family during terrible times and more to be congratulated than condemned. But the tale finished sadly. By the time poor van Meegeren began to serve the one-year sentence the courts imposed he was so weakened and demoralized by his ordeal that he fell ill and died, without ever having had the chance to develop his talents and sign his work with his own name. After the forger's death, as a final irony, a rush of van Meegeren fake Vermeers began turning up in unlikely places and under odd circumstances. It seems there were collectors ready to pay substantial prices for a genuine van Meegeren fake Vermeer, and lots of artists in chilly Amsterdam garrets were happy to fill the demand.

Critics and experts react to successfully floated forgeries with the same kind of outrage I felt at the purloined Bonnard image in the hotel spa, and seem to take it just as personally, possibly because they themselves are shown up as having been gullible or too easily deceived, and large sums of money are involved. Fifty years after the *affaire* van Meegeren,

Thomas Hoving, curator, art historian and self-styled "fake-buster" wrote a very different version of the story in his book *False Impressions*. Van Meegeren didn't fool any of the real art experts, Hoving says, just the careless, the arrogant and the sloppy. He speaks of van Meegeren's work with the abhorrence most of us save for something we've stepped into on the sidewalk, calling it putrid, awful, rotten, disgusting. Van Meegeren was a Nazi sympathizer, he says, a cheat and a thief whose only talent was for copying, and whose early death was due not to his having been ill-treated by the Dutch or the courts and prisons, but to his lifelong addictions to alcohol and morphine.

The British master forger Eric Hebborn really was an artist. He was born in 1934, a penniless youth who soared through England's most prestigious art schools winning scholarships and awards at every stage along the way. He could draw like an angel. He claimed to believe that the worth of a work of art was determined not by the author's signature but by the quality of its execution, and that a forger whose paintings are equal to those created by Old Masters is not a criminal. He reserved that term for the expert or the dealer who was in it for nothing but the money. He was no blundering van Meegeren. He never made a claim for the authenticity of one of his own drawings unless a recognized expert made it first, so the misattribution always rested squarely on someone else's shoulders. Fooling those experts was his special skill, but he said his moral code forbade his getting at one of them when his acumen was down or forcing him to make a quick decision over a boozy lunch. The more competent and well-known the victim, the more he enjoyed his scam. Among the connoisseurs who certified his forgeries was another master of deception, Hebborn's friend and lover Sir Anthony Blunt, curator of the Queen's pictures, art expert and lifelong spy for the Soviet Union.

Hebborn deceived everyone for nearly twenty years, watching his work pass muster with museums, dealers and auction houses all over Europe and the United States. Canada was not left out. The National Gallery in Ottawa acquired a group of 17th-century drawings by Stefano della Bella that turned out to be Hebborn forgeries. Thomas Hoving angrily dismisses Hebborn as one who had never lifted his works above their "plodding, sloppy, insubstantial, forced academic essential nature," but after Hoving set himself the test of choosing between two Corot drawings — one the original and the other a Hebborn copy — he reported with satisfaction that "I had, of course, been right" — which sounds like an admission to the possibility of his having been wrong. In the flurry of activity after Hebborn was unmasked large numbers of recently acquired drawings in museums and important collections were pulled as fakes or doubtfuls, when, according to Hebborn, many of them were good as gold and not his handiwork at all — which would suggest that either the experts were shaky in their judgements or Hebborn was a better forger than anyone cared to admit. Of course, Hebborn may have been lying once again. Being exposed for what he was did Hebborn nothing but good. He was never prosecuted by the museums and collectors and auction houses that were his shamefaced victims, and he was now besieged by shady dealers who would pay him twelve hundred pounds a shot if he could "find" drawings by certain renaissance artists for buyers they had ready and waiting.

For all the candour and charm of Hebborn's memoir and the air of bonhomie that evidently inspired so much unearned trust, somebody had it in for him. One night in 1996, while he was sitting on a park bench in Rome, an unknown assailant crept up from behind and struck him a fatal blow on the head with a hammer. My outrage at the painting in the hotel spa would hardly fuel that kind of violence, but I just might go back one day and aim a spitball at it.

When I consider my own feelings for the work of Pierre Bonnard I don't think a forger could possibly love — even truly admire — the work of the artist he's copying. You don't desecrate what you love. It's more likely that such a person checks out what's hot in the art markets and picks what he thinks he'll be able to fake convincingly. It's hard to imagine that Hebborn couldn't have produced genuine works of art if he'd wanted to and if getting rich quick hadn't been his main goal, but in spite of his specious arguments on their behalf his forgeries are as shoddy as my studio-mate's overworked reinterpretations and van Meegeren's fake Vermeers. Maybe all three simply lacked the spark that ignites an artist's imagination, the aesthetic intuition that has nothing to do with thinking or calculating and without which no amount of cleverness or fine technique can produce a work of art.

The question is not how skilfully a painting or drawing has been done or how well it represents its real-life subject, but how well it expresses the artist's unique apprehension of that subject. In *Art and Illusion* Ernst Gombrich included a section about copyists and forgers, whom he said can never produce anything worthwhile because they are not working from the vocabulary of forms an artist develops over years of study and practice and from which his own unmistakable personal style has emerged. An artist is not trying to recreate the object or the scene before his eyes but to make an account of seeing it. Cézanne wasn't concerned with the apples he painted again and again but with his perception of those apples, and that's what distinguishes the artist from the copyist — the copyist is only concerned with the apples.

Unmet Friends

Some years ago a friend gave me a copy of Carolyn Heilbrun's memoir *The Last Gift of Time, Life Beyond Sixty*, as a (very appropriate) birthday present. I found so much to agree with and enjoy in that small volume that I went on to read more of what she had written. Heilbrun, who was a scholar as well as a writer in several genres, thought that being older is liberating for a woman, because if you no longer care what people think there really isn't much anyone can do to you. In another book, *Writing a Woman's Life*, she said perhaps it is only when they are old that women can stop being what she called "female impersonators," begin to make use of their newfound sense of security and take risks. She thought old women should make noise, be courageous and engage in work that required them to learn.

If they were to follow her advice, women would have to turn their attention away from the practical matters that have probably commanded it for most of their lives and follow the paths to where imagination and half-forgotten dreams might lie. I was at an advanced age when I set out to write my first book, a small memoir about my mother's life, but before me as a model and inspiration was the English writer Mary Wesley, whose work I had read and admired since the appearance in 1983 of her first novel, *Jumping the Queue*. Wesley was seventy the year that book was published, living proof that getting off to a late start did not preclude becoming a published author. Wesley was to me what Carolyn Heilbrun has called "an unmet friend," someone known and admired, even loved, through the one-way correspondence of her work. Heilbrun herself became another of those unmet friends, as was the writer Margaret Laurence, whom I finally did get to know briefly when I painted her portrait in 1983. The fictional characters in the novels these women wrote, as much as accounts of their own lives, raised issues and posed questions that helped me make sense of my own.

An achievement less easy to measure than the writing of that first book was for me the shedding of a gnawing conviction that in pursuing my own interests I was doing that which I ought not to have been doing and neglecting what I ought. In my younger days what steps I took toward self-expression were faltering ones, unconsciously calculated, I believe, to be just enough to keep my hand in without actually becoming engaged as a player in the larger games of life and taking my chances out there among the pros. My early passion for painting developed into a spare-time activity that didn't take on a professional status, with real exhibitions in real galleries, until after my fiftieth birthday, while my published writing had consisted of occasional lightweight newspaper articles about keeping house and looking after a family, and later a few columns of art criticism.

At the close of World War II it had seemed as if something new and extraordinary were being held out to young women of my generation, a promise that they would from now on be able to participate in the wider world to a degree unknown to their mothers and grandmothers. It was suddenly no longer a rarity for women from middle-class families to attend university, go on to graduate school, even apply for training in professional fields like engineering and architecture that had always been virtually closed to them. For most, the promise was one unkept. Women like me took their degrees, got married, had children, and proceeded to lead lives at least as narrowly defined as their mothers' had been, apparently accepting that this traditional role must, after all, have been what they'd really wanted all along. Heilbrun observed that women have always been told that the "safety and closure" of marriage were what was best for them, and that a woman's true happiness lay not in first-hand engagement with the larger world, but through the man at the centre of her life.

But fulfilling the needs of others is no substitute for living your own life and developing your own talents, and I can't think of any simple answer as to why women continued to do it through the fifties and sixties and seventies and to some degree even up to the present day. In the beginning, right after the war, we were all grateful to the thousands of returned veterans who had already lost years out of their lives, and they unquestionably deserved the best of what was available in the way of jobs and educational opportunities in whatever field they chose. But there was something else. During the war women had done difficult and important work and done it well, but now there was a subtle backlash that quietly began to undermine the strength and independence that had put women in administrative posts and behind the wheels of trucks and in factories building airplanes. I can only suppose that when men returned home from overseas they were disturbed at how the social structure had changed while they were away. Perhaps they felt they had lost an ascendancy they believed was their birthright, and it made them anxious.

Whatever it was, women's ambition and desire for independence was twisted and warped until it became a moral issue: real women, good women, would not want to compete with men in the workplace or anywhere else. I remember feeling uneasy and even ashamed about my own aspirations toward being an artist or a writer (who did I think I was?) before I'd even decided what kind of artist or writer I wanted to be. I couldn't have put a finger on the source of those feelings, but looking back I think it was everywhere — in the jokes that were told, the movies we watched, the postwar fashions that emphasized generous curves and tiny waists, the widespread perception that the desirable women were always endearingly ineffectual if not downright stupid — and after hearing often enough and from so many different quarters that ambition in women was uppity, and that displaying intelligence and business acumen made them unfeminine, unattractive, *bad*, women began to believe it themselves. Anger was an unfeminine emotion, so we sublimated it into a pseudo-spirituality that played up the "feminine" virtues of selflessness, doing good works and putting the needs of others before our own. We wanted men to love us. When we were angry we said we felt "hurt." You could almost say we did it to ourselves.

As girls entering adulthood at the close of the war, Carolyn Heilbrun and Margaret Laurence didn't buy it, and were already beginning to pit themselves against the societal strictures that appeared to most of their coevals, myself included, to be as immutable as laws of nature. If I didn't quite swallow this doctrine hook, line and sinker, I at least took a good bite out of the bait, and when both women wrote later of their loneliness, their rage, and the endless frustrations — accompanied, always, by that miasma of shame, the guilty sense that in pursuing what they believed they were destined to do they were failing as *women* — I recognized belatedly the anger and frustration I had felt myself. Heilbrun believed that ambitious women make men feel less than manly and want women to be different from them in more than the obvious ways. She observed that one of the myths generated by a patriarchal society was that a woman's ambition beyond the traditional female role didn't come from inside, as it did with a man, but somehow invaded her from without. The desire for worldly accomplishment was as foreign to a woman's real nature as a disease, and if she was any kind of a woman at all she would refuse to succumb to it.

Laurence and Heilbrun were both born in 1926 and I myself the following year, so I know well the tenor of the times in which they grew up, and the possibilities for women were substantially the same whether you lived in Manhattan or Neepawa or Toronto. Like me and most of our coevals both of those women married young, both loved their husbands and children, but Laurence needed to be a writer and Heilbrun, although also a writer, needed, or was convinced that she needed, to become part of the mainstream academic world, where she believed, naively perhaps, that study and research are aimed at uncovering truths that have nothing to do with gender. Each encountered tremendous difficulties for no other reason than that she was female. After Margaret Laurence had become a renowned author she wondered if she might in any way have been a "half-assed pioneer," a model for other women, but as Heilbrun has written, male-dominated society has always chosen to see accomplished women as abnormal, egregious exceptions whose successes were due either to luck or the generosity and good will of others, rather than to their own talents and hard work.

Margaret Laurence committed suicide with an overdose of sleeping pills after being diagnosed with terminal cancer when she was sixty. Carolyn Heilbrun was in good health — if one bent on suicide can be said to be in good health — when she took her own life at seventy-seven. She had written earlier that death was not something negative when it was a controlled choice. Unlike these two, Mary Wesley was still writing until shortly before her death of natural causes at ninety. Perhaps her longevity and vigour were due to her having taken up her pen late, when the high-octane fuel of her most deeply felt emotions and experiences had not yet been consumed in the fires of creation. Looking back on her remarkable literary career, Wesley said in an interview that she had no patience with people who decide to grow old at sixty, that it should be the time to start something new, and she asked herself ruefully why she had not done more with her life from the very beginning.

To one who grew up in the monotonous provincial city Toronto was when I was young, Wesley's childhood as a member of a wealthy upper-class family, ensconced in a fine house in Windsor Great Park and attended by servants and governesses, sounded fabulous, the setting for a romantic English novel. In fact it was an unhappy one. She described herself as overlooked and lonely, the youngest of three children, whose mother actively disliked her and whose father she seldom even saw. Any envy I might still have felt for her circumstances dissolved when I read about the scrappy education her family provided for the brilliant and imaginative girl she must have been. In comparison to my years at high school, university, and finally an art school, Wesley received virtually no education at all. Since it was expected that she would never have to work she was tutored at home by foreign governesses, from whom she learned little beyond something of the languages they spoke. After that she was sent to a Swiss finishing school where marketable upper-class females were given a final polish before being presented at court. After that they were expected to catch good husbands while the bloom of youth was still upon them.

Wesley did what was expected of her — married a lord ten years her senior, bore him two sons, endured their loveless union as long as she could and then scandalized her family by leaving him. During the war she found a new freedom and sense of independence by doing intelligence work in London, in an atmosphere she described as one of "terror and exhilaration." At a party one evening she met the love of her life, a twice-married German-Irish playwright and journalist named Eric Siepmann, and cut herself off forever from her parents by moving in with him until both could divorce their respective partners and marry. The couple settled in a large house on Dartmoor and Wesley bore a third son. She appears to have spent the rest of her years with Siepmann as a fulfilled and happy wife and mother, caring for her children, keeping house, gardening, cooking, knitting, and looking after the family pets.

In 1970 Siepmann died, leaving his widow feeling, she said, as if she'd been cut in half like a carcass at the butchers. To compound her grief, Siepmann, who had changed jobs frequently, left her with virtually nothing to live on. With a son still in his teens to raise and educate, she sold the beloved house on Fernworthy Reservoir where she had lived with Siepmann and raised her three boys and moved to a tiny house in the village of Totnes. She taught French until it was discovered that she had no qualifications as a teacher, worked in an antique shop, flogged her jewellery and valuables, took orders for knitting. She had dabbled at writing for years, but finally, with the encouragement of her friend Antonia Fraser, she decided to try in earnest to become a novelist.

Before her first manuscript was accepted it was turned down by half a dozen publishers who said no one would want to read a story in which a female protagonist is full of anger, uses language a lady ought not even to have in her vocabulary and indulges in sexual behaviour inappropriate to her age and social position. In 1982, however, when Wesley was seventy, the first of her ten novels was published, of which all subsequently became best-sellers and three were dramatized for television. By the time she died at ninety ten million copies of her books had been sold worldwide. Of her late start as a novelist, she said she hadn't suddenly been inspired to become an author in her old age, as people seemed to think, but had for years been trying to teach herself to write and tossing the unsatisfactory results of her efforts into the wastebasket.

Wesley was so devastated by her husband's death that the thought of committing suicide crossed her mind, and she used the memory of that impulse when she wrote her first novel, *Jumping the Queue*. Her protagonist, Matilda, recently widowed, penniless, and all but estranged from her self-centred children, can see no reason for going on living. She plans to have a little picnic of wine and cheese at the seashore and then drown herself in the outgoing tide, but her plan is frustrated by a series of incursions and mishaps. Disloyal friends are re-encountered, her husband's incestuous relationship with their daughter comes to light, clandestine drug smuggling activities are revealed, past transgressions remembered. Matilda finds solace in a brief sexual affair with a man fleeing from the police. After he departs, she again packs a picnic basket, and at the conclusion of a story in which the spectre of death hangs over every page, successfully drowns herself.

Novelists write themselves and those who have affected their lives into their stories, satirizing them, trimming their characters to fit the plot, idealizing or demonizing them as it suits their purposes, and allowing them to express emotions and desires their creators might not reveal in their own lives. Carolyn Heilbrun created an alter ego in Kate Fansler, the protagonist of her series of mystery novels written under the *nom de plume* Amanda Cross. Margaret Laurence unquestionably inhabits several of her female characters, but probably most of all Morag, in *The Diviners*. There is always humour in Wesley's work, often in the form of deliberately not-quite-believable coincidences and amusing chance encounters, but beneath the apparently casual acceptance of incest and murder, the conveniently overheard conversations and the cruel if amusing bitchiness of aristocratic Mayfair matrons, lies a dark and angry emotional substratum where violence and rage, feelings of vindictiveness and memories of betrayal lie buried. In more than one of her novels there is an unloved and lonely girl trapped among snobbish aristocratic adults whose elegant manners conceal a baseness of character.

The foundations on which Wesley constructed her stories were people from her own background, her memories of wartime London and the southwest part of England that she had come to love. When her books began to bring in substantial amounts of money she moved to a slightly larger house in Totnes, but otherwise wealth changed little in her life. She probably deplored the arrival of a supermarket and the housing estates that were beginning to sprawl out into the countryside, but in Totnes, as in almost all of England, past and present are on a visible continuum.

I spent a few days in Totnes once. Its steep cobbled high street is lined with crooked Tudor buildings that house tea rooms and china shops and those old-fashioned labour-intensive English provisioners where one person cuts and weighs the piece of cheese, a second takes the customer's money, and a third hands over the wrapped package. The River Dart runs through town, rising and falling with the tides. Each day a small excursion boat plies its way downriver between rolling green hills to the ancient port of Dartmouth, and a few hours later, when the moon pulls another long streamer of the Atlantic ocean deep into the Devon countryside, the boat comes puttering back up to Totnes. It seemed to me the quintessential civilized and self-contained ancient English town. There are multitudes of stories about artists and writers who go chasing all over the world looking for a place to call home, a corner of the planet where they can live and work and feel they belong, but when Mary Wesley took up her pen, she was already there.

I never saw her in person, but the author photograph on several of Wesley's books shows in profile the face of a handsome, aristocratic-looking woman with a still-firm chin, finely shaped nose, an arched brow rising over a deep-set eye. Her white hair, what can be seen of it, is becomingly swept back and tucked behind her ear; on her head she wears a large, wide-brimmed felt hat. Her beautiful clothes of silk or cashmere and her reserved demeanour were both commented upon by interviewers and even in her obituaries, but in her writing she was not reserved at all. When challenged during an interview about the strong language she put into the mouths of some of her characters, she replied, in her elegant upper-class accent, that "fuck" was a perfectly good Anglo-Saxon word.

I remember standing in front of a mirror carefully adjusting a new (and required) hat on my twenty-two-year-old head in preparation for a ladies' club luncheon laid on by my prospective mother-in-law, wondering, momentarily, if I had turned some sort of corner in my life and would have to dress *properly* from now on. The hat phase soon passed, and as a wife and mother I wore trousers for all occasions, with the exception of funerals, at a time when most women were still sticking to skirts. It was the mildest form of rebellion. If my outer accoutrements said "free spirit" they cloaked a woman who half-knowingly concealed who she was, even from herself, for the first five decades of her life. Until the latter third of the twentieth century, the way women dressed and wore their hair and made up their faces more often than not failed to reflect the unacknowledged person within. They were Carolyn Heilbrun's "female impersonators."

Mary Wesley lived almost all her life among the artifacts of generation upon generation of the fair-skinned race whose origins and customs, culture and language she shared, and who had called that same small land home. For Laurence and Heilbrun it was different. Apart from the dwindling native population, we citizens of the New World are all in a sense displaced persons, still looking beyond our own shores for an understanding of our cultural heritage and ourselves. We are footloose, perennial roamers and shifters-around in our own vast territories. I am convinced that many, if not most of us, live with an unexamined awareness in some deep level of our hearts that our place of birth was arbitrary and home is elsewhere.

Like Morag Gunn, the female protagonist in her novel *The Diviners*, Margaret Laurence couldn't wait to escape the narrow confines and puritanical mores of the prairie town where she was born, and although the place clutched at her soul until she finally exorcised it in her last novel, she knew from an early age that she hadn't been brought into this world to spend her life in Neepawa, Manitoba. But if the place where one was born is not home, then where on earth is it? When Laurence was young, she imagined it might be in Scotland, land of her paternal forbears, the fantasy of a Scottish idyll that appeared in the stories and songs of Morag's adoptive father Christie in *The Diviners*. Later she said she was "mock Scots," no more Scottish than she was Siamese, but just the same she ascribed the dark side of her nature to the half of her heritage that was "black Celt." A short time before she died she arranged to have bagpipes played at her funeral, a lament from that small distant land to which many fourth and fifth generation Canadians feel so strong a mystical attachment that great numbers of them don kilts and eat haggis on Robbie Burns day.

Margaret Wemyss was twenty-one when she married Jack Laurence, a man ten years her senior whom she herself said might in some way have been a substitute for the beloved father who died when she was nine. The couple moved first to England, then to Africa. During those years Jack Laurence professed to admire the writing his wife managed to squeeze into her busy days as wife and mother, happy to read her manuscripts and offer criticism, but little by little Margaret came to realize that his opinions were not helpful but in fact the reverse, and that he was jealous of the time and attention she gave to writing. The marriage had begun to founder.

Her situation was one which, if not entirely peculiar to her era, was much exacerbated by it, that of the talented, intelligent, university-educated woman trying to balance the traditional female role she felt obliged to undertake with a vocation she could not ignore. For Laurence's generation, as for previous ones, the word "woman" was job description as much as gender, and she was never able to exempt herself from its implications. Of her double life as wife and mother on one hand and writer on the other, she continually asked herself whether she had the right to the second if it took up the time and energy owed to the first. She tried to do it all, clean and cook, care for her children, iron her husband's shirts, be his companion when he was home and still obey that overwhelming compulsion to write. One life or the other seemed always to be getting shortchanged.

The creative urge was not something she could continue to defer. It would have taken more self-discipline than she could have mustered not to write. She said that when circumstances kept her from getting down to writing about a theme or a character that was racketing around in her brain, it drove her almost mad. Artists appear to be born with a condition — either a deficiency or an overabundance of some psychic ingredient — that is as compelling as any chemical addiction, and to tell a born writer that she should forget about making up stories and lead a normal woman's life is the equivalent of telling a heroin addict he ought to just buck up and stop using the stuff. What made Laurence's situation even harder to bear was the knowledge that men in general, and her husband in particular, didn't have to face this dilemma, and it fuelled a rage that boomeranged back on her as unbearable guilt for her inadequacy as a woman.

She came to understand, finally, that she had to write, because unless she did she had no identity. She said she could only be certain of who she was when she became someone else, speaking through the mouth of the characters in her stories. So write she must, but she could no longer do it as a married woman. When Jack was offered a contract in Pakistan in 1962, she decided not to follow, but instead took their children to England, first to London, and then to a house in the Buckinghamshire town of Penn. There Laurence was able to raise her children and find more time for writing, but she lived in isolation and loneliness. Neither the locals nor the well-to-do Londoners who rusticated there — people she described, according to her biographer James King, as "an accumulation of snotty Tories" — were much interested in a displaced lone female who spoke in the plain accents of small-town western Canada.

To add to her problems, engineering contracts were becoming scarce for Jack and Laurence was obliged to assume more and more responsibility for supporting herself and her children. Her books and articles were by this time being published, so with what came in from her writing and dwindling assistance from Jack, she was able to meet expenses, but in letters to her literary "tribe" back home, she spoke again and again of her overwhelming loneliness, and after almost a decade in England, of her growing desire to return to Canada. As a first step she bought a small cottage on the Otonabee River near Peterborough, which eventually became the setting for *The*

Diviners, and in 1973 she upped-stakes for good, sold her English house and settled into a stolid and rather graceless brick house in the town of Lakefield, Ontario, that bore a more than passing resemblance to her grandfather's house in Neepawa.

I had for many years maintained with Laurence the one-way friendship between reader and author that Carolyn Heilbrun said endures forever because it is never bridged, never tested, but a bridge appeared one evening when I met Margaret Laurence at a party in Peterborough, and I crossed it. I asked her if she would allow me to make a few drawings of her, which, if they worked out, might evolve into a portrait, and she generously agreed. She liked the portrait, and when I offered it to her she accepted it as a gift, as I insisted, in return for the wisdom I had received from her books. It was our last meeting.

Margaret Laurence's heroines seem to me less the creations of a careful observer and student of character than beings who evolved from within herself, created out of her own substance. They inhabit real women's bodies whose rhythms and fluctuations and desires they can no more control than the River Dart commands the tides that fill and empty it. They are loving mothers, dutiful daughters, helpmeets who struggle to fulfil their roles, but they are also intelligent human beings with real minds, and her novels are chronicles of the efforts of those women to gain some measure of control over their own lives. They were an inspiration to me.

After she was diagnosed with terminal lung cancer the doctors sent Laurence home to wait out the progress of the disease, but she decided to save her children and herself a prolongation of sorrow and pain, and with what seems to have been her practice of doing the hard jobs first, she chose to take a shortcut to the inevitable with an overdose of sleeping pills. It was a brave and reasonable act, one for which I would hope to have the courage under the same circumstances. In her last hours she made a few final entries in her journal, writing with what seems to have been a feeling of bewilderment that mostly what she had done with her life was write books, but why she had written them she no longer knew, nor why it had seemed so important to her to do it. In another entry she asked her dear ones to forgive her, and I wondered if she were asking to be forgiven for committing suicide or for having had that compulsion to write that made it impossible for her to be ordinary.

The Margaret Laurence whose portrait I painted was a plain, stout woman in her late fifties, little resembling the slender satin-gowned bride of the wedding photograph reproduced in Lyall Powers' recent biography. The day I made my sketches she wore baggy dark slacks and a blue turtle-necked pullover, no makeup; her eyebrows were unplucked and black-rimmed glasses magnified her dark eyes. The woman I saw was the woman she was, Margaret Laurence the writer, and it is to be hoped that her great success in that role compensated at least in part for the difficulties she met along the way. Perhaps it was not on mere whim that she gave the protagonist of her most autobiographical novel the name "Morag" — a pet form of the Gaelic "Mór," meaning "great."

Photographs of Carolyn Heilbrun taken while she was an undergraduate at Wellesley show her wearing clothes that would have been interchangeable with my own when I was a student — prim pleated tartan skirt, white Peter Pan collar lying neatly over the neckline of a long-sleeved pullover. Heilbrun was into her late middle years when, with the encouragement of her grown children, she began to exchange the lady-professor's knitted dresses and suits, creeping pantyhose and crippling pumps for flat-heeled shoes and trousers, shirts and tunics that she bought from catalogues. Her body by then had become what she described as a shapeless bolster that she had given up trying to starve into submission. Her biographer Susan Kress says that in her middle years Heilbrun "deliberately aged herself" by hauling her curly graying hair back into a bun and dressing carelessly, but perhaps it was less a matter of aging herself than arranging things so the inner woman and the outer one jibed. Heilbrun resented having been obliged to wear *de rigueur* academic drag during her earlier days at Columbia, and she said that in any case, no matter what she'd worn, it was only because she was married that she was spared the smirking imputations of lesbianism directed by her male colleagues toward the few other women on staff, on the premise that those who chose to invade a male preserve were probably queer in more ways than one.

During the years when she was working toward her doctorate at Columbia and later when she was taken on staff, Heilbrun said she was chronically torn between voicing her real thoughts, which might have come across as controversial and "unfeminine," or keeping her mouth shut and giving way to the opinions of her male professors and peers. "Men had declared," she wrote, "that a woman who tries to take on a male activity is no longer a woman, and that the characteristic which is mostly unwomanly is ambition." I was re-reading her 1997 memoir *The Last Gift of Time* when I was stopped in mid-line by a sentence that began with the words: "Is it that I suspect that had I been wholly successful as a woman ..."

What in God's name might a successful woman be, I wondered, if Carolyn Heilbrun didn't qualify? She was by then past seventy. She'd had a long and apparently happy marriage to a man she admired and loved, and who, from what she tells us of him, loved her back. She bore three children, raised them to sane and healthy adulthood, saw grandchildren arrive. She was one of seven out of her Wellesley class of four hundred and seventy-eight to go on to earn a Ph.D. She was instrumental in bringing down barriers erected against women at the leading university where she was a tenured professor and was revered by her students. She wrote not only respected academic works, books, essays and treatises, but also a widely read memoir, an important biography, and the hugely successful series of Amanda Cross mystery stories to which in the early days she dared not attach her own name, lest being the author of works of popular fiction should prejudice her acceptance at Columbia. Her words seemed to disparage everything she had achieved, and yet after a moment's reflection, I understood what she meant. She had been taught early in life what our generation could never entirely unlearn — that women's strength lies in their "ability to appear helpless, and their success in inspiring male lust," as she put it, and in "the selfless service they provide for others." These were the criteria by which women were to measure their success.

Heilbrun was in her sixties when she walked away from her hard-come-by tenured position at Columbia, remarking afterward that it had been a shock to find out how little she missed the "poisonous atmosphere" of that academic world of which she had struggled so hard to be part. Now she took pleasure in time spent "without a constant unnoticed stream of anger and resentment, without the daily contemplation of power always in the hands of the least worthy, the least imaginative, the least generous." She said that the old boys at Columbia would have thought it was the end of civilization if they had been required to admit more women and blacks. Heilbrun wasn't black, but she was Jewish, a fact she chose to regard as being of no importance in the progress of her career. But it was no secret that Wellesley maintained a strict quota for the admission of Jewish girls and a classmate of Heilbrun's said of her that although it was never mentioned and they were all very polite about it, everyone was aware that she was Jewish.

At Columbia, where Heilbrun completed a master's degree and doctorate and was later taken on permanent staff, anti-Semitism was not even politely concealed. Lionel Trilling became one of Columbia's great names, but even he had been told, in reference to his newly granted tenure, that he was not to regard it as an invitation to bring in more Jews. Heilbrun said if his name had been Cohen instead of Trilling he probably wouldn't have been admitted at all.

Heilbrun's mother had believed that to be Jewish was to be "lower class." She disliked being Jewish herself and had wanted her husband to change his name so they could "pass," which may explain why her daughter ignored the handicap of being Jewish in that actively anti-Semitic milieu and concentrated instead on the more obvious drawback of her femaleness. In the early days she was more concerned with getting admitted to the male-dominated academic world herself, than with breaking down those barriers for other women. Later, after she had achieved tenure and had begun to argue against the whole sexist and racist set-up at Columbia, she was seen by her colleagues as having exceeded the limits of what was tolerable. That she was female and Jewish had been bad enough, but when she came out as a feminist she found herself virtually ostracized.

If she had supposed that other female professors at the university might become allies, she was mistaken. In those days women who had squeezed through the barricades and established themselves in male preserves, dissassociated themselves from feminists like Heilbrun lest they be seen as tarred by the same brush. It was safer to hang in with the boys, even if it meant they had to tolerate innuendos about their sexuality and be objects of scorn for their single status in a world where an unmarried woman was no woman at all. At a time when females constituted an underclass, their loyalty to one another was secondary to their social, political and sexual success with the dominant males on whom their positions and welfare depended. Heilbrun remembered how unmarried female professors at Wellesley had been looked upon by her fellow students as "sexless" and "failed" because they hadn't managed to catch husbands. She made few friends at Wellesley and fewer at Columbia. She remarked that she began to have real friendships with women only after she left university life entirely.

Until the feminist movement was under way Heilbrun had never been able to put a name to what it was that had aroused her anger even as far back as her undergraduate days at Wellesley. At Columbia she set out to become a critical authority on English literature but found herself gradually sidetracked by "the huge unfairness that riddled the system" — racism, anti-Semitism, and the automatic assigning of women to a second-class rank. The controversial questions that interested her were seen as a threat to the power and privilege her male colleagues had always enjoyed, and, predictably, were dismissed by them as trivial and unworthy of academic interest. Nevertheless her writing and research began to follow a course away from studies of English classics and literary theory to the less narrowly defined fields of women's place in literature and the arts, and contemporary feminist issues within and beyond the walls of academia.

Home, to Carolyn Heilbrun, was for most of her life one or another of a number of large comfortable apartments overlooking Central Park in Manhattan. There was no shortage of money, either before or after her marriage. Her well-to-do father, who had arrived in the United States as a penniless immigrant, had dreams for his only child, and she did her best to fulfil them. Heilbrun's biographer Susan Kress says that Heilbrun's father "deracinated" her by concealing from her all knowledge of the members of his large extended Russian-Jewish family living in the United States, denying her the sustenance she might have derived from her ethnic and religious roots. She was a serious hard-working student who never developed an interest in the small avocations with which both men and women leaven and add variety to their hours on earth — cooking, sewing, gardening, decorating and furnishing the apartments she lived in with her husband and children. She didn't like parties or ethnic food or travel — unless the travel took her to England, the country in whose literature her mind had been steeped. Apart from her affection for dogs and cats, her interest in nature seems to have been scant.

I had not known before I read her memoir that Carolyn Heilbrun and Amanda Cross, author of a series of mystery stories, were one and the same. Cross's characters were more wordy than witty, and all seemed to speak with a similar mannered and erudite correctness, but the stories were unique in that they starred a female private detective twenty years before mystery writers such as Sue Grafton and Sara Paretsky created theirs. Heilbrun endowed her protagonist with attributes she would clearly have wished to have herself. Kate Fansler was a slim, blond, beautiful WASP, elegantly dressed and happily single for most of her career. She was, like Heilbrun, a tenured professor, but freely independent and under obligation to no one. When she finally did marry, it was to a man who was frequently away in the far corners of the earth, and married or not, when Kate ran into an ex-boyfriend, she hesitated mere moments before spending the night with him. Unlike Heilbrun, who lived the schizophrenic see-saw existence of a mother who was at the same time deeply engaged in a professional career, Kate was childless.

Heilbrun wrote that she had pretended to be part of two worlds, the gentile and the male, but that she belonged to neither. I think she was wrong and "pretended" was the wrong word. She really did belong in those worlds and she helped to reconstruct them. Because of women like Heilbrun places of learning in western countries can no longer justify the exclusion of otherwise qualified candidates who happen not to be white or gentile or male. She described herself in her memoir as a sometime-melancholic and perhaps she was in that state when she took her own life. It's a shame that she chose to leave just when the battle was won. Similarly Margaret Laurence, for all her self-doubt, was much more than the "half-assed pioneer" she hoped she'd been. She was an exemplar, a leading Canadian writer of her time of either sex and one of the few whose works are still, nearly two decades after her death, on every library shelf and in every bookstore in the country. Mary Wesley wouldn't qualify as a half-anything either. Double would be more like it.

As for me, I have two lives running simultaneously, one as a septuagenarian very much aware of the brevity of life and the other as a person who becomes so engrossed in putting paint on canvas or juggling words on a computer screen that time and age become completely irrelevant. The two reintegrate themselves to some degree when the latter attempts to translate into images or words what the senses of the first have recorded. One half of me may occasionally feel the slowing effects of time but the other half can't wait to get at whatever the current project may be. So I rise eagerly from my bed in the mornings and spend my days engaged in serious work that requires me to be courageous, and in which progress can be seen and measured. I listen to people who are younger than I am, and learn from them. I take risks. I make noise.

Speaking Italian
like a Canadian

We were half way through our first visit to Italy when I said to my husband, "I'm coming back to this country and between now and then I'm going to learn to speak the language." That was in April of 1957, the beginning of a lifelong love affair with Italy and all things Italian, a more-or-less undeclared yearning to run away and spend the rest of my years in what must surely be the most beautiful and welcoming country in the world. Vowing that I would learn the language was a vain boast. Generous gifts were bestowed on me by the Creator, but an ear for languages was not one of them.

I was at that time the thirty-year-old mother of three young children, a third-generation Canadian through whose veins coursed thin Anglo-Saxon blood, a child of the depression who came to adulthood during the Second World War when foreign travel was off limits for everyone. Before that journey I had never been off the North American continent — nor, indeed, had my parents before me.

When I was young the names of Italian cities like Pisa, Florence, Venice, Rome sounded as mythical to me as Samarkand and Shangri-La. Italy only began to be a real place for me when large numbers of Italian immigrants came to live in Toronto after the war. My gray old city bloomed: wrought-iron balconies replaced dowdy wooden verandas on brightly-painted house-fronts; Italian cafes spilled out onto sidewalks where old men sat sipping fragrant coffee in the spring sun; bounteous displays of fruits and vegetables appeared outside the shops of Italian greengrocers in summer — phenomena we buttoned-up Torontonians had never seen before. We ventured into aromatic shops that sold cheese cut from vast wheels; we were introduced to anchovies packed in barrels, to salami and prosciutto and different kinds of olive oil. We learned that pasta wasn't necessarily a baked casserole of macaroni and cheese or a plateful of mushy canned Heinz spaghetti. We tried cooking things we'd never seen before — and sometimes we messed up. On her first attempt to cook zucchini my mother-in-law rendered the delicate vegetables inedible by throwing them into a pot of water and boiling the bejasus out of them. For the present generation it must be difficult to imagine what an un-cosmopolitan lot we Torontonians used to be.

I took to walking in the new Italian neighbourhoods so I could eavesdrop on conversations in the shops and cafés and grocery stores. The language was unintelligible to me but it rippled with musical cadences and I loved listening to it. I picked up the occasional Italian newspaper, read the signs in the stores and the menus in cafés and tried rolling words quietly around on my tongue — *farfalle, melone e prosciutto, gelato fresco. Marcello Mastroianni. Incidente automobilistica.*

On that first adventure back in 1957 we had entered the country from the north, planning to spend the first night in Udine and then making haste to fabulous Venice. The weather had been cold and wet for days and the mountainous terrain through which we had driven was bleak and forbidding. Then all at once, as we crossed the border into Italy, the skies cleared miraculously, the sun shone and the rolling country-side looked so green and lush we felt as though we were descending into the promised land. The attitude of the Italian customs agent was reassuringly informal after all the stone-faced heel-clicking correctness we'd encountered during the previous leg of our journey. The man handed our passports back through the car window with a smile, wished us a happy journey and waved us on our way. This was my kind of place. I felt as if I'd come home.

I walked into the Piazza San Marco with an English-Italian phrase book in my hand, but words in any language, including my own, would have failed me. My first sight of the cathedral, the banners, the campanile and the glorious vast piazza was so overwhelming that I stood there gaping, open-mouthed, feeling as if my heart could scarcely bear the weight of such splendour. I think a person can be starved for beauty, just as one might be starved for some essential nutrient in one's diet, without ever being aware of it.

We left Venice reluctantly and went on to Florence, where once again there was too little time and much too much to absorb. We emerged from our *pensione* early each day and returned to it late, dizzy with fatigue, overwhelmed, a pair of mute, glassy-eyed tourists who couldn't open their mouths except to mumble *buongiorno* or *grazie* when the occasion seemed appropriate and the rest of the time managed to mispronounce everything they tried to say.

As soon as I was back in Toronto I enrolled in a one-on-one course in conversational Italian at a Berlitz language school and on our next trip to Italy I knew enough words and constructions at least to make my wants known, if in a stumbling manner. Between the many trips back in the decades that followed, sometimes with my husband and sometimes on my own, I made sporadic attempts to improve my fluency by taking courses at various institutions or private lessons with Italian speakers, buying records and the accompanying books that guaranteed to make me bilingual in a matter of weeks. The trips multiplied. We went back to Venice, visited Rome. One summer we sailed from Corfu across to Brindisi, drove up the Adriatic coast to Ravenna to see the early Christian churches in one of which, if I were God, I would certainly choose to dwell. On another trip we drove down from Rome to Napoli, prowled the lost city of Pompei, set out in early morning for Paestum and stood gazing in wonder at the sight of Greek temples casting long shadows on the dew-beaded grass.

As the journeys multiplied my efforts to speak Italian continued. I could make my wants known in a hotel or a shop but comprehending what other people said to me was still a problem. Enough of these Mickey Mouse courses, I decided. Twenty-odd years after that first visit I flew by myself to London and thence to Pisa and spent an entire month in Firenze, the mornings at a language school in the Piazza Santo Spirito and afternoons following an art-history professor through the Duomo and various churches and monuments and piazzas, listening while he expounded, slowly, and in beautifully articulated language that even I could understand, on the wonders of the Italian Renaissance. Before the month was over I took a day trip to Siena and to my surprise was able to carry on a simple conversation with an Italian woman sitting beside me on the train without having to mentally translate every word before I opened my mouth.

I was in my mid-sixties when a half-Italian Toronto couple offered my husband and me a month's holiday in their villa overlooking the valley of the Bormida in Piemonte, in exchange for a painting that I would execute during our stay and of which the motif was to be something from the breathtaking Piemontese countryside. As soon as we arrived I stretched a canvas, set it up on an easel on the terrazzo and went to work, doing what I was born to do in the country I felt I should have been born in. A few days before our visit was over we were invited by a neighbour to help with the grape harvest. I worked in the rows with several other women, cutting the bunches of grapes and dropping them into plastic bins, finding myself at last able to converse in Italian, shaky Italian to be sure, but comprehensible. Since that matchless September I have had the good sense to decline the couple's invitation to return to that wonderful place, in case the second visit should in some way blur the remembered perfection of the first.

I had already passed my allotted years of three score and ten when we flew to Genoa and boarded a ship that carried us down the Mediterranean coast to Palermo. There we hired a car and made a leisurely trip through and around Sicily. We climbed the Scala in Caltagirone, looked out over the ramparts at Enna, gazed with awe at the archeological wonders in Taormina, Selinunte, Siracusa, Agrigento. We spent a day at Piazza Armerina and then, by way of a rest, settled for a few days in the unpretentious city Sciacca. I fell in love. I found my Italian home.

Our *pensione* was a few steps from the main piazza with its views of mile upon mile of the angular shoreline that recedes into the distance until sky and water and land blend into a haze of indigo and violet. Directly below the piazza, at the bottom of a steep cliff, winds a ribbon of white road lined with palm trees where parked cars look as small as ladybugs. Houses cling to the steep slope in overlapping layers of red tiled roofs and honey-coloured walls, with palms and orange trees tucked here and there on tiny patches of ground between. Oleanders and geraniums bloom on the balconies and lines of laundry flap and bleach in the sun.

I went out onto the piazza on a Sunday morning before the bells began to ring for mass and soon a number of elderly men, pinkly fresh-shaven and dressed for church, came drifting out onto the piazza to promenade slowly up and down in groups of three or four, hands clasped behind their backs, leaning toward one another to speak, cocking an ear to catch what was being said. Some sat on the wrought iron benches, smoking and talking politics, receiving serious attention and affirmative nods from their friends. I perched discreetly at the end of one of the benches with my sketchbook, conscious of being the only woman in what was evidently a male preserve on that particular day and hour.

A shadow fell across my drawing pad; one of the men was standing beside me, watching me draw. He asked where I was from and when I told him his face lit up. He told me his nephew had gone to Toronto to work. "Will he ever come back, do you think?" I asked. He looked surprised. "Of course he will. He still owns a house here, and some orange trees. He'll come back when his children are grown up, when he's finished working." The churchbells began to ring just then and he moved on to rejoin his companions.

I strolled into the upper part of the old city, an easier walk on a Sunday morning than during the busy weekdays. Shafts of sunlight were cutting between the tall old houses and laying brilliant yellow bands across the cobbled roads and on the stuccoed walls. I passed a tall wooden door standing open in an otherwise blank wall. Through it I could see part of a sunny paved courtyard where a few plump white chickens clucked behind wire netting; geraniums bloomed in terracotta pots set about on the brick paving. A wooden staircase led up the side of the building in stages to what must have been three separate apartments, one above the other, and at the top, from a tiny rooftop balcony, pink bougainvillea came spilling down the ochre wall. A rooster crowed; my heart filled with longing. I wanted to stay here for the rest of my life, live up there in that topmost apartment, eat my breakfast on that balcony in the morning sun, look over the red-tiled roofs and across the piazza to the sea.

I have an Italian-born friend here in Toronto, a fellow artist. Sometimes we go to exhibitions together and she patiently allows me to converse with her in Italian. When she speaks, though, poetry sings through her words; she uses those elusive subjunctives so foreign and difficult for the English tongue, a mode that conveys a sense of might-have-been, of longing and possibility. What she says, sometimes, seems less important than the way she says it. Compared to hers, my speech is as flat-footed as a business letter.

I may, *nel cuore*, be an Italian, but I will never sound like one.

Magari.

Less is Enough

If I lean dangerously far out over the railing of the third-floor balcony of the house I can see the dark crown of a purple beech whose branches spread dense shade in the little park at the foot of the street. During the past twenty years I have observed that tree in all seasons, examined it up close, run my hands over its smooth hide, even measured its girth. I've made drawings of it during its spring budding before the limbs disappear into foliage the colour of eggplants; I've made paintings from the drawings. The main trunk, which is now eight feet in circumference, looks as though it were bulging with barely contained muscular energy, like the columns of the early Greek temples at Paestum. Here and there people have carved initials and names into the smooth blue-gray bark that is more like a skin than bark, some of them incised so long ago that as the tree has grown the letters have blurred and risen high out of human reach. At its base, where that massive trunk emerges from the earth, it is encircled with short humped projections like elephants' toes that dig purposefully downward rather than sprawling casually just under the soil, as do the roots of neighbouring trees.

The largest of the three major limbs springing from the trunk is as big around as the hot water tank in my basement. I don't know how old this particular specimen of *Fagus Sylvatica Purpurea* is, but such a tree can live for two and a half centuries or more, and reach a height of a hundred feet. This one was undoubtedly planted in the late nineteenth century when these narrow inner-city streets were being built up with rows of tall narrow brick houses, long before the park itself came into being or the twenty-storey apartment building on its southern perimeter was so much as dreamed of.

A small river used to flow here, winding through the park and the terrain on which the apartment building stands, meandering across the present Bloor Street and down through the grounds of the university, making its way southeastward across downtown Toronto to empty into the lake. As the city rose and pavements were laid down the stream was driven underground, trapped and tamed and confined to pipes and sewers. It has been banished from sight, but perhaps the roots of the beech tree still draw water from that underground stream. I'd like to think so. Unlike some of the acacias and soft maples hereabouts the beech shows no signs of aging. Every spring it leafs out in full glorious symmetry with not a twig left bare as far as I can see. The tree is in its prime. Entropy may take its toll on the Victorian houses as the years roll by but they are continually being restored and renovated, re-roofed and rewired, painted and parged and pointed, made shipshape for yet another generation of householders. As for the people who plant trees and build and restore the houses, life is short. *"We blossom and flourish as leaves on the tree, and wither and perish …"*

We human beings deteriorate rapidly and none too prettily and soon cease to exist, but our own and other people's bodies are of consuming interest to us, and to none more than artists. While Sigmund Freud peeled away layer by layer the neurotic defenses of his subjects, his artist grandson Lucian Freud strips the clothing from his and scrutinizes the aging bodies of his models with meticulous, pitiless, intensity. Freud says he underplays the faces of his subjects because he wants the expression to emerge through their bodies; for him a head is no more important than a limb. In his portraits breasts sag and bellies bulge; legs are netted with veins, genitalia are empurpled; the arms and legs of some are plucked-chicken scrawny while others are drooping with rolls of fat; necks are puckered, faces and hands are blotched. If young people didn't already know that the pleasure they take in their own physical beauty is one of nature's practical jokes, these nude studies would make it evident. Freud's imperfect bodies are depicted with such unrelenting realism they make me flinch and almost want to look away, but as works of art these paintings express something beyond surfaces, a kind of nobility, the courage to endure in the face of physical deterioration. It ain't over 'til it's over, they seem to say. I saw Freud's double portrait of an aging man and woman lying naked together in what might be post-coital sleep and found it so poignant it brought tears to my eyes.

I have a clear memory of pumping up a steep hill on my bicycle at the age of thirteen or fourteen and passing on the way a gray-haired woman who was walking slowly up the same hill carrying a bag of groceries. She was probably all of fifty-five and fit as a fiddle, but I thought, as I sped past her, that such a feeble old person must be envying me my youth and the wiry strength of my legs, wishing she were fourteen again, whizzing along on a bicycle. Since then I have discovered that many of the things I can no longer do I no longer want to do, that the pleasures of youth are supplanted by new and even better ones previously unimagined. Writing a book requires more endurance and is a lot riskier and ultimately more rewarding than riding a bike up a hill. These days my own body would be a good subject for one of Lucian Freud's paintings. I don't care to appear in public in a bathing suit anymore, let alone be seen naked. One of my hip joints is wearing out and will soon have to be replaced, but, as they say in Italy, *non è cancro*.

Every now and then there's a television clip of some ninety-eight-year-old man who holds down a full-time job bagging groceries in a Florida supermarket, but such robust individuals are few and far between. We hope for a long life, since the alternative is not appealing, but a body with enough years on it starts to break down like an old flivver, requiring more and more frequent repairs and departing farther and farther from whatever the current ideal of beauty may be. I have wondered if Carolyn Heilbrun stepped out of the shower one morning and caught one glimpse too many of her nude person in the bathroom mirror. Could the unacceptability of her body have been one of her reasons for rejecting existence itself? She believed the life of reason should end in "rational" suicide, which is not to be confused with the escape taken by those who have lost the will to live or are motivated by fear or illness, but is rather a free, and above all intellectual, choice. She subscribed to the philosophy of the Roman Stoic Seneca, who said it is the quality of life that matters, not the quantity, that just living is not a good thing, but living well. A wise person "lives as long as he ought, not as long as he can." Seneca taught that a morally and intellectually perfect person will not be affected by passionate feelings that arise from false judgements, which sounds just fine if it can be managed, but if the pursuit of this moral and intellectual perfection leads to suicide, who is left to aspire to wisdom or feel passion or make judgements of any kind? Cutting the process short by ending life itself seems to deny the validity of the entire enterprise. Mortal illness aside, I believe that if we find the quality of our lives unsatisfactory, it is up to us to change them.

In *The Last Gift of Time* Heilbrun wrote of her appreciation for a sixth decade of life that had been, to her surprise, happy and productive, but the gifts bestowed on her early decades were scarcely mean. Her creative talents automatically placed her among the world's blessed, and even keeping in mind the Stoic principle that material advantages are not "goods" but merely "preferred things," she was the cossetted, brilliant, only child of well-to-do parents who were eager to provide for her intellectual development, a rare advantage for a woman in those times. She was reported to have been in good health when she jumped the queue and made her exit at the age of seventy-seven, the same age, perhaps significantly, at which her mother had died. If she had waited another hour, another day, another week, might she not have felt an unanticipated surge of joy arising from something as simple as the turning of the autumn leaves in Central Park, some glimpse of happiness that would have made her say *Not yet, not yet*. Before she swallowed her sleeping pills or pulled the plastic bag over her head — both methods of self-dispatch were mentioned in the media — Heilbrun is reported to have written a note to her husband and children saying "love to all," as though she were writing them a postcard from abroad — which in a sense I suppose she was.

With the exception of those few fortunate individuals, the "once born," as William James called them, who come into the world wholly and authentically themselves and remain that way, with no need in later years of spiritual epiphanies or painstaking analysis of their psyches to find out who they are and where the hell they went wrong, it takes most of us the better part of fifty or sixty years to grow up, and unless a person is facing a certain and painful death it does seem counter to his or her best interests to cut short that eye's twinkle of time between the attainment of maturity and the onset of senility, during which further insights and revelations might well provide previously unimagined forms of happiness.

I have tried to visualize Heilbrun alone in her apartment that last morning, taking a bath, brushing her teeth, combing out the curly gray hair and pinning it up again, looking through her wardrobe for something appropriate for the occasion, lining up the pills and the plastic bag and finally sitting down to write that goodbye note. She had decided to do it earlier rather than later, it seems, because she was afraid if she waited too long she might lose control and not be capable of carrying it through. It was as though she were undertaking a final exam, for which, if she got everything right, she would be awarded an "A." The newspapers reported that she may have been suffering from that catch-all disorder called depression, but perhaps it was the reverse side of the coin, maybe she had never learned in all her seventy-seven years to feel the joy that Paul Tillich has called "the happiness of the soul," that affirmation of one's essential being toward which Seneca's prescription for the moral life was also directed, which makes the desire for honours in any worldly undertaking meaningless.

I will maintain my physical self — the part of the human unit St. Francis called "Brother Ass" — in as good working condition as possible and try to focus my attention elsewhere. It's my turn to watch (without envy) as the fourteen-year-olds go whizzing by on their bicycles. I've enjoyed living in this house, but the time has come to move along and set up housekeeping on a more manageable scale. I will soon move into an apartment in that twenty-storey building on the other side of the park. From the balcony there I will have a closer view of the great copper beech and will draw it again, in various seasons, from a different perspective to be sure, but not a less interesting one.

Before moving day the *stuff* must be thinned out and pared down. I have descended upon my bookshelves with a certain glee; the survivors of my draconian weeding will be those books I am sure I will read again. New ones will no doubt come sidling onto the elevator and up to the apartment and through the door to pile themselves on top of one another in the shelves, but for the time being the few keepers will be enough: the reference and art books, the Nabokovs and the Annie Dillards (a book by one of those two will likely be prised from my lifeless fingers at the end), the works of Joyce Cary, V. S. Naipaul and the wonderful Henry Green, from whose novels Graham Greene once said he had learned what good writing was. I'll keep a few English classics, some books of poetry and the three-volume annotated Shakespeare, so that when my grandsons call for help with their English homework I can sound as if I know what I'm talking about.

Joyce's *Ulysses*. I will finish it yet.

I believe that living well means staying awake, looking and listening, noticing things. Time and habit conspire to dull perception of what is close at hand. We take for granted that what we are expecting to see will be there when we take the trouble to pay attention to it, and are surprised when it isn't. I took a good look at Sheba recently and discovered that the dog I think of as just out of puppyhood has become gray around the muzzle. How long has this been going on? Unless one continues to hone awareness as the years pass, habits of mind will make the *now* not worth bothering with, while attempts to repeat outstanding past experiences lead to comparisons that disappoint. The old things aren't as good as they used to be, the present seems unwelcoming, and the future belongs to somebody else.

I don't order bouillabaisse when it's on the menu because my mouth remembers the ambrosial dish I ate on a sunny terrace in Marseille thirty-odd years ago. I saw Fonteyn perform *The Firebird* at Covent Garden once, and I don't need to see it performed again. But it isn't extraordinary long-ago events that blunt perception of the present, it's the entrenched routines, the fixed opinions and attitudes, the comfortable cop-outs of mind and body that eliminate the need for thought or decision that will find us rearing bolt upright on our deathbeds, belatedly aware that we've spent this precious gift of time sleepwalking.

Elevation

Horizon:
The line at which the earth and sky appear to meet. The line at which the earth and sky would appear to meet but for irregularities and obstructions.

OED

Moving into an eighth-floor apartment has given me a new perspective on the world. The entire north wall of my new living room is made up of floor-to-ceiling windows that offer a panoramic view of the city and a great sweeping expanse of sky. It's like living at the top of a high hill. From my new viewpoint at treetop level that arbitrary line at which the earth and sky appear to meet is now much lower than it used to be and my days up here are at least half an hour longer than the ones I've been accustomed to. I am still watching the last glimmerings of the sunset when all below has faded into night.

All that daylight pouring in was disconcerting at first, and I would enter the room on even a dull morning with my arm bent above my brow as one shielding mortal eyes from the splendour of a heavenly visitation. But I am accustomed to it now, and the sky has become the object of the kind of scrutiny I used to reserve for terrestrial things. What I once regarded as a patch of emptiness between the treetops or a wedge of blue separating the roof of my house from the one next door I now see as something substantial, a lively scene of continuous activity where everything changes so dramatically with each passing moment that to turn one's back on it is to risk missing some interesting and important event.

I have discovered a way to study a stretch of sky all on its own, untethered from the earth. Beyond the apartment windows there is a deep balcony with a masonry wall running along its outer side, and if I slouch away down into the low sofa facing the windows I am able to isolate a wide band of pure sky between the upper edge of that wall and the overhanging roof which is the bottom of the balcony above. Having gazed at it in the early morning and at midday and at dusk and sometimes during the small hours of darkest night, I see that the sky is full of things — clouds of every shape and texture, airplanes, flocks of star-lings and various birds that fly solo, flurries of autumn leaves, air-borne plastic bags, helicopters, stars and moon and sun of course, but also spots of light that I now know are planets and others that are

man-made satellites cruising through space. I can follow the flight of mosquito-sized silver airplanes glinting in the morn-ing sun and watch their twinkling progress after dark as they enter my viewing space from the east, bank around a broad curving trajectory and head westward again toward the airport, descending gradually until they disappear below the horizon, or, as the OED would have it, below the irregularities and obstructions — in this case trees and buildings — that conceal the place where the earth and sky would appear to meet if I were able see it.

On wet days gulls move up from the lake and fly slowly past my windows, turning their heads this way and that on the lookout for abandoned sandwiches. Against clear blue autumn skies hawks float above the city with quietly spread wings, circling and circling on rising currents of air. One morning a helicopter from a TV station thudded past so low and close it made my windows rattle and I could see the man at the controls. Some day a hot air balloon may come drifting past, its basket full of ladies and gentlemen who will salute my startled self with raised champagne glasses.

Kindergarten-art clouds go shipping across my viewing screen on a bright afternoon. They are in a continuous process of metamorphosis, splitting like amoebas every few seconds, leaving pieces of themselves behind, recreating their shapes en route. Here comes a whale with a big round eye that almost immediately transforms itself into a dog with its tongue hanging out, and then, as it begins to move offstage, bulges up in the middle and stretches its neck to a ridiculous length. Do you see that cloud that's almost in shape like a camel?

Finding animals in cumulus clouds is all well and good, but a little basic research teaches me that given suitable conditions those apparently harmless fair-weather puffs of cotton can develop into the towering cumulonimbus associated with thunderstorms, that hurricanes can result from gigantic

swirlings of them, and furthermore, if they should become suf-
ficiently twisted by the wind they might turn into tornados,
at which point my dog Sheba and I and I would be off to the
Land of Oz. When I was checking out cloud types I was particularly taken with one called the mammatus, a not-particu-
larly-attractive pouchy gray formation that looks like a mattress with its stuffing falling out, but the name has a nice mater-
nal connotation, and although it may look ominous the mammatus is entirely unthreatening and usually appears after the
thunderstorm is over.

I deduce, belatedly, considering the many years I've
been observing my surroundings on this planet, that sky without the context of the terrain below gives no indication either
of season or region, and the patch of it I have isolated would
be unremarkable on a blazing summer day in Piemonte or a
perishing cold winter one in Calgary or during any season of
the year in Barbados or Denmark or Samarkand. As I am enjoying my flash of empirically arrived-at knowledge a tiny smudge
appears in the lower left-hand corner of my skyscape. The
smudge becomes an upside-down check-mark which moments
later resolves itself into a skein of geese coming this way, heading south. Soon I can distinguish individual birds, see their
wings beating, watch the odd one shift laterally and flap on
alone for a second or two before moving back into formation. I could happily watch them all afternoon, but in a few
minutes the whole show has passed over my head and disap-
peared from view. So much for my recently acquired wisdom.
This piece of sky must be over Canada, and the season can be
none but autumn.

When I rise from the sofa the horizon drops and the
sky reattaches itself to Toronto. The immediate neighbourhood of small streets lined with cheek-by-jowl Victorian houses
(including the one from which I recently moved) is so thickly

treed that only the occasional peak of a slate roof or an egregious brick chimney appears among the scarlets and russets and
ochres of autumn foliage. The upper branches of two nearby
Lombardy poplars where congregations of inky grackles spend
the afternoons establish a foreground in the composition
framed by my windows. The more distant cityscape, reading
left to right, begins with a nearby jumble of nondescript apartment buildings rising out of the banks of trees, and above them,
farther away on the crest of a steep hill that cuts laterally across
the city, are the crenellated towers and ramparts of Sir Henry
Pellatt's folly, Casa Loma. Next, out of another wide band of
the ubiquitous autumn forest juts a faux-Tour Eiffel communications tower adorned with red lights to warn off news helicopters and balloonists. A few sugar-cube apartment buildings
a mile to the north sit at the edge of Sir Winston Churchill
Park (rechristened from the more prosaic Reservoir Park after
World War Two) through which a narrow tributary of the Don
River flows sluggishly at the bottom of one of the deep ravines
that mark the city's topography.

Imposing office towers and condominium buildings on
St. Clair Avenue stand guard across the top of the hill and
march eastward to rendezvous with assorted high and medium-
rise buildings at the corner of the north-south thoroughfare of
Yonge Street, where they turn right and descend the incline in
serried ranks. Halfway down is the verdigris dunce-cap roof of
the clock tower on the old North Toronto CPR railway station, a rather handsome building that was closed for business
soon after the much larger Union Station was erected downtown on Front Street. The Prince of Wales (later to become
the Duke of Windsor) officiated at the opening ceremonies
of the new station in 1927. "You build your stations like we
build our cathedrals," said the prince, ungrammatically. The
old North Toronto station recently underwent a reincarnation

as the world's only liquor store with forty-foot ceilings and antique brass ticket-wickets at the checkout, not to mention new works in the clock my father referred to as a four-faced liar. I have the vaguest recollection of disembarking at that station with my parents — or was it just that I heard them talking about having done so themselves? If the memory is not a false one I was at most three years old at the time, so either my recall is phenomenal, or they were still allowing passengers to disembark there after its official closing in 1930, or the whole episode is a fantasy I dreamed up so I could say to my grandchildren, "See that liquor store that used to be a railway station, kids? Well, when your grandma was young, etc." It is rumoured that the now-redundant Union Station is itself being considered for recycling as a shopping arcade or venue for rock concerts. Paris turned its old Gare d'Orsay into a splendid art museum, but there you are.

That steep hillside that cuts laterally across Toronto was once the shoreline of the ancient posthumously-named Lake Iroquois that was scooped out by glaciers some thirteen or fourteen thousand years ago. When ice jams in the St. Lawrence River finally broke loose, the vast volumes of water that had been pouring over the Niagara escarpment found an eastward outlet to the Atlantic Ocean, and Lake Iroquois slowly diminished until it settled more or less into its present configuration as Lake Ontario. In the lowlands near the shores of the new lake a dense hardwood forest sprang up around a natural harbour that was eventually to be the site of a British settlement called York.

Lieutenant Governor Simcoe decided that York (later renamed Toronto) was a propitious spot for his provincial capital, so he called upon surveyor Joseph Bouchette and his corps of army engineers to mark out roadways through the untouched wilderness. Faced with a piece of territory that included the curving shore of Lake Ontario, two large rivers fed with myriad streams and tributaries and the steep hill that marked the shore of the ancient lake, they seen their duty and they done it. The paper they used for their charts was flat, after all, and ruling honest straight lines was one of their best things. Lakeshore and hill, lowlands and heights, rivers and ravines be damned, they drew up their plan as for a featureless plain. They ignored all the winding paths the native people had followed along the river banks and the shores of the lake, took no notice of their meandering routes that allowed for gentle ascents of the hill. The straight-lines-right-angles grid was marked out in the army measurement of two-kilometre chains, which didn't begin to make sense until Canada adopted the metric system nearly two hundred years later.

They did accommodate their master plan to the topography in just one instance, and then only slightly: the sloping north shore of Lake Ontario lay roughly twelve degrees off the horizontal, so they set the rigidly straight base of the master plan accordingly, thus forever shifting all the city's streets off the true points of the compass and making it appear that the sun here rises in the southeast and sets in the northwest. When a river or stream disobligingly got in the way of the grid they buried it when they could, or failing that threw a bridge across it, and if neither was possible discontinued the road and picked it up again on its far side. There are still streets in Toronto that allow a ravine the right of way by coming to a dead end on either side of it. In this central part of the city the forest appears to have prevailed, though, in spite of the best efforts of those surveyors to curb it.

My view from up here is Olympian, purified of imperfections. I do not see the filthy sleeping bag and empty bottles under a bench in the park where a homeless man dosses every night,

or the waste container
spilling over with pop
cans and plastic wrap-
pers and reeking bags
of doggy-doo that I
know is there too. I
can't tell from up
here that the water
that comes splashing
from two high jets to
fill the foot-deep wad-
ing pool looks less than
clean. I can't smell the
exhaust fumes belching out
of the cement truck that's making
its laboured way up Bedford Road followed

closely by an impatient city bus and three cars, and the sound
of its grinding engine is much muted. Distance lends to the city
the aspect of having been tidied to have its picture taken, all
neatly arranged and colourful and interesting, an idealized version of the real thing.

When I set about drawing what I can see from these eighth-
floor windows I decide my sketch should include a portion of
the interior of the apartment as well — an indoor-outdoor
motif I often choose that once drew a wry observation from my
younger son who asked, "Can't you get out, Ma?" With charcoal pencil in hand I assess what lies before my eyes. The bottom edge of my paper will cut across the room at a level that
takes in the back of a wicker rocking chair, a potted benjamina
tree, the far half of a round wooden coffee table, one end of a
sofa, and what I can see of the dog, Sheba, who is lying at the
moment on her green mat next to the windows, watching me

with unconcerned eyes. The balcony and its railing run behind all that, beyond the balcony my cityscape and above the city a band of sky.

The two Lombardy poplars growing in the park at the foot of this building rear up higher than the hill that was the shoreline of Lake Iroquois, higher than the turrets of Casa Loma and the communications tower and the apartments and office buildings that crown the hill. There's a potted amaryllis on the coffee table that was supposed to be a Christmas plant but got started early, and now the tops of the two foot-long stems that shot upward out of the bulb have exploded into eight enormous scarlet flowers that would look more at home in a Brazilian jungle than posed against the background of Toronto in autumn. The tops of the flowers are at the level of St. Clair Avenue. There are a few streaks of high cirrus or cirrostratus cloud at some twenty thousand feet up in an otherwise clear blue sky, and against them are silhouetted the lacy branches of the benjamina tree that made the transition to the new apartment without dropping its leaves, as those trees are wont to do. It reaches the full height of the windows, considerably higher than the poplars, and its breadth is such that it takes an airplane the size of a gnat almost a minute after disappearing into its thickety foliage to emerge unscathed out the other side.

Out there, buried among those colourful autumn treetops, is the horizon to which everything in my drawing relates, the line where the earth and sky would appear to meet but for all the irregularities and obstructions that conceal it. Apart from the angles of the nearest of the blocks of apartment buildings it is difficult to see how all these things pertain to that horizon, because the forms I'm drawing are so disparate and their lines of intersection so irregular. But I am looking down on the top surface of the coffee table, which means it must be below the horizon, while the top of the amaryllis plant must be above it because from where I sit I am looking at the undersides of the blooms. At some point on the way up, those two thick green stems are intersected by the line of an invisible, immaterial, non-existent horizon.

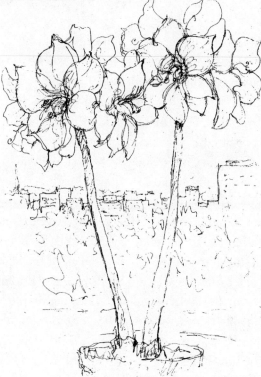

Life Study

I've been looking with renewed interest at a work that's been hanging on my living room wall for the past twenty-odd years. It's a drawing by the late Erik Loder, a painter and consummately talented draughtsman whom I knew during the dozen years I lived in the country near Peterborough, Ontario. The work is executed in black crayon on white paper, with a few strokes of red and some smudges of violet to emphasize roundness of contour and areas of shadow. The model is a young girl who stands turned away from the viewer, so the right side of her face and one breast and the gentle curve of her belly are in profile. In the three-quarter view of her back, both shoulders and the elbow of the far arm and all of the near arm can be seen. Her muscles are supple-looking and unexaggerated, the hips slim, buttocks rounded. A few lines on the lower part of the drawing represent folds of drapery, as though the model had allowed a wrapper or gown to slide down to below her hips where she now holds it against either thigh with her hands.

But there's more. Within the figure's outline Loder has drawn and shaded in parts of the girl's skeleton — the neck bones, the vertebrae of the spine, the bones of the nearer upper arm and forearm and the neatly articulated projection of the elbow; a shoulder blade, a slab of ribs, the pelvis where it joins the lower end of the backbone — all without any sense of the macabre or feeling that the work was intended sardonically as a memento mori. When I bought the drawing from Erik all those years ago I asked him if, during the course of his studies in New York, he'd been required to work from the skeleton and from those flayed figures that expose the musculature of the human body. He replied, "Of course," sounding surprised by the question, as though such exercises would have been part of any art-school curriculum. He went on to say that he included bones in many of his life-studies because he particularly liked drawing them, and after all it was the bones that gave the body its form, the way foundations and beams are what give its final shape to a house.

Bones have been very much on my mind lately. If I were to use Erik's fanciful simile and liken my own bones to the foundations and beams of the fleshly house in which my spirit dwells, I would say that the building had begun to go askew, that the beams and foundations were showing signs of deterioration that was causing a sagging and a listing and a painful grating of the hinges.

A specialist I consulted told me the problem was one that had to be taken seriously: the supporting timbers were no longer sound or true and the whole edifice was being thrown out of kilter. No makeshift propping-up would do, either. The place was old, in case I hadn't noticed; in real-estate lingo it would be called a heritage property. Things were not going to right themselves on their own, either. What was happening now could only get worse, and would certainly do so if the situation were ignored. Fortunately there were modern methods for restoring old frameworks like mine. A rotten beam and joist could be cut away and discarded and a metal jack and other parts installed in their place to set the structure in line again. In his skilful hands and with the use of the best modern materials the renovations would last — quick glance to check my date of birth — my lifetime.

At the clinic they took x-rays and parts of me I'd never seen before — or what I was told were parts of me, I wasn't convinced they hadn't mixed my pictures up with someone else's —

were put up on the computer screen. Severe osteoarthritis of the right hip, the only cure: total hip replacement. *Total hip replacement?* Whoa there! Just a darn minute! Yes, of course I'd been having discomfort walking, that was why I was here. All right, severe discomfort. Yes, I suppose you could call it pain. Getting into the car was a bit of a hassle but I'd gotten used to lifting the leg with both hands and hauling it in after me so that wasn't a real problem, but I would admit that climbing the stairs was becoming a pain in the neck, I mean the hip. The man in charge tapped on the screen with a pencil. Look. See. Right there. The cartilage has all worn away, the lubricating juices have dried up, the hip socket and the ball on the head of the femur are all frayed and scruffy. The joint's worn out. What you've got there is bone grating on bone.

When I got home I did some Internet research about the surgery I'd just agreed to undergo. I turned up what looked to be a reliable article on the subject, but found I couldn't read it all at once without breaking out in a sweat and having my hair stand on end, so I downloaded it and decided to absorb it in gradual doses over a period of time.

The steps for replacing the hip begin with making an incision about 8 inches long over the hip joint. After the incision is made, the ligaments and muscles are separated to allow the surgeon access to the bones of the hip joint. Once the hip joint is entered, the femoral head is dislocated from the acetabulum. Then the femoral head is removed by cutting through the femoral neck with a power saw.

The brochure showed the parts in question in the form of simple diagrams. I imagined the details for myself — the clamps and vises, the pipe wrenches and hacksaw blades, the spattering blood and the bone chips flying through the air.

I don't know with any degree of accuracy how the bones of the human body articulate with one another, where the muscles attach, how an arm or a leg works. My artistic education, unlike Erik Loder's, was somewhat hit and miss. Much as I love drawing and painting the human figure, my knowledge of its mechanics is rudimentary and any skeleton I might draw would look like a decoration for a kids' Halloween party. A lot of paper still gets wasted when I draw and much trial and error lies buried under layers of paint on my canvases. During my early student days I learned a few schemas for making parts of the body look plausible, like sectioning off a basic egg shape for a head and getting the features in more or less the right places by setting the eyes half way between crown and chin. I recall being taught in high-school art classes how to measure a standing figure into an appropriate seven or eight "heads," to put a man's navel at his waist and a woman's a little lower on the abdomen, to have the legs account for half the average person's height. The classrooms were full of live human beings of which any one might easily have served as a model for the rest, but at that early stage of our artistic education few if any of us were ready for drawing from life. We hadn't learned the language yet, did not know how to reconfigure in our heads what our eyes were seeing and translate it into intelligible marks on the paper. Arriving at that level takes a great deal of study and practice.

If you give a three-year-old paper and crayons and ask him to make a picture of a tree he doesn't run to the window to look at the maple on the front lawn, he draws what he already knows about trees and produces a green lollipop on a brown stick. It would be nice to think that all budding artists have to do is grab pencil and paper and learn everything they need to know by looking at what's in front of their eyes, but before a painter can even begin to develop an individual style by which his work may later be identified, he has to bring the overwhelmingly complex natural world under control by devising and storing up a repository of abstract templates, like the child's lollipop tree. In his book *Art and Illusion* art historian and theorist Ernst Gombrich quotes Nietzsche, who said that since nature can't be subdued by the artist, he chooses from it what he likes, and paints that. And what does he like? Why, what he knows how to paint — which will be the things that have caught his attention and he has developed the skill to represent — like Erik Loder with his figures and bones.

... special rasps are used to shape and hollow out the femur to the exact shape of the metal stem of the femoral component. Once the size and shape of the canal exactly fit the femoral component, the stem is inserted into the femur ... the stem is held in place by the tightness of the fit into the bone (similar to the friction that holds a nail driven into a hole drilled into wooden board — with a slightly smaller diameter than the nail).

Gombrich calls it the modern dilemma that the developing of a schematic vocabulary has been thrown out of art-school curricula, leaving the artist high and dry. High and dry, and, one might add, as blissfully free as a toddler on the beach flinging sand in every direction. The old *sine qua non* of the artist as being someone who knows how to draw has been tossed aside. "Creativity" (a word that makes me flinch) is thought to lie within every breast, and for those who can't discover their own vein of the precious lode there is no shortage of workshops offering to give the process a kick-start. What Umberto Eco calls an "orgy of tolerance" is in mode, a bland all-inclusiveness that lacks even the wryness of Dada or the irony of camp.

Those in favour of the kind of painting that makes no reference to the visible world argue that the work itself is an object in the visible world and as such is not required to represent or even refer to anything else. Fair enough, but curators and gallery-owners and artists themselves seem unwilling to leave it at that. Lest the work and the circumstances of its conception be misinterpreted they print up and post alongside it lengthy tracts about the artist's philosophy, his intentions and his psychic state at the time of painting, often in language so turgid as to make one wonder if it's actually about the painting in question. One such commentary doesn't necessarily jibe with the next. Barnett Newman's jumbo tri-colour canvas *Voice of Fire* in Canada's National Gallery was described in the accompanying literature as "an objectification of thought that floods our consciousness with a sublime sense of awe and tranquility," while elsewhere the same painting was said to represent "the anguish of man's abandonment." Take your pick.

When there are no clues as to what the artist wanted the viewer to take from a work, everyone who looks at it will dredge up something from his own experience and project it onto the painting, deciphering its forms as mattress ticking or flying tiddlywinks or a chicken's viscera. If that kind of subjective reading was the artist's intention, fine, but if he really wants to get his own point of view across it's no fair breaking into print to do it. There's a whole world out there for him to weld his ideas to, whether it be forms from nature or esoteric icons or commonplace objects, like the pots and bottles Giorgio Morandi managed to infuse with so much mystery and metaphysical meaning. Cézanne chose apples and a blue-and-white ginger pot and the faceted slopes of Mont Ste. Victoire as the framework for his formal discoveries, probably for no other reason than that he enjoyed painting them. I doubt whether artistic talent, where it actually exists, is so fragile a flower that it shrivels under exposure to diligent instruction. The compulsion to make art is not easy to repress or divert, and it would be better, I think, to have mastered a repertoire of schemas and procedures against which to rebel, or to revise to suit one's needs, or in the end discard altogether, than to be cast rudderless into a sea of benign permissiveness.

… In the uncemented variety of artificial hip replacement, the metal shell is simply held in place by the tightness of the fit or with screws to hold the metal shell in place …

Among my late mother's childhood keepsakes (she was born in rural Ontario in 1901) I found a doll, a baby's form reduced to the simplest of schemas — seven round wooden balls of graduated sizes strung together on a cord, with a tiny ball on either side of the largest one for ears. The toy is of a size to fit small hands and it bends and nods just enough to give it a semblance of life and motion. It has no arms or legs as such — this baby is obviously swaddled so the bottom end of it comes more or less to a point, like Popeye's "adoptid infink Swee'Pea" — and the face has no features unless you count those ears, but even a tiny child would know what it represents. We project what we want to see, which is most often an image of our own kind, and we manage to find it on the moon or on the knotty trunk of a tree, a decayed masonry wall or in a blob on a toasted cheese sandwich. Perhaps all earthly creatures seek others of their own species to reassure themselves that they're not alone in the universe — like my dog who becomes exhilarated at the sight of another dog a hundred yards away across a grassy field. I am no exception. When a human figure appears in a work of art, even a tiny one in a very large painting, to it my eye flies first. I'm with Auden who wrote:

> To me art's subject is the human clay
> And landscape but a background to a torso.
> All Cézanne's apples I would give away
> For one small Goya or a Daumier.

Lucian Freud admits to harbouring a little of the Pygmalion fantasy, a barely conscious hope that some day one of his painted figures might actually come to life. He has said that when it becomes obvious that a work close to completion is turning out to be just another picture after all, he feels let down. If ever a painted figure were to draw breath and step down off the canvas it would be one of Freud's, but probably most figurative artists feel a little God-like when a new work is getting under way, when the image is still immanent and the painting can become almost anything wished for. If actual life can't be imparted to a painted figure there can be another kind of life in the work as a whole, an aesthetic quality that infuses it with electric energy. When Erik Loder wasn't drawing his eloquent half-transparent nudes he turned his attention to what was growing in his garden and drew huge cabbages that were ready to burst, or sprawling clumps of rhubarb shooting their seed-stalks skyward with such force one could almost hear them screech.

You now have a new weight bearing surface to replace your diseased hip. The therapist will carefully instruct you on how to avoid activities and positions which increase the risk of hip dislocation.

The structure now requires only the support of a single flying buttress, and even that becomes less and less necessary as weeks pass. Until recently I never gave a thought to canes or the people who carried them. My father sported one in his younger days for purely ornamental purposes — during the thirties a slender brass-ferruled cane was a dandyish Burlington Bertie accessory to be swung forward and allowed to hit the ground only at every other step — a balletic manoeuvre that distinguished the debonair from the disabled. My father-in-law on the other hand, whom I knew only in his later years, was a serious walker, and would sally forth on a brisk four or five mile hike of a Sunday afternoon having made a selection (usually a gnarled blackthorn) from an assortment of sturdy walking sticks kept in a polished brass stand in the vestibule. Now that the snow has melted and we of unsteady step are able to venture out of doors I'm surprised to note that I pass half a dozen other cane-users during a stroll of only a few blocks, many of us women and all of us vintage to a greater or lesser degree. There's a sort of camaraderie among cane-users — we nod to each other or raise our walking sticks in greeting as we pass, perhaps saluting one another's continuing mobility.

Hopefully, you can expect 12-15 years of service from your artificial hip.

That ought to do it.

When I was a young child at the Loretto day-school in Toronto, Mother Maureen used to lead our grade four class in prayer each morning, asking God for the quick release from purgatory of the soul that was closest to heaven. We were convinced of the strength and effectiveness of our supplications, certain that if we all prayed like sixty the transfer would occur immediately, with a sound like a popping cork. After a long cold Toronto winter my whole being yearns for spring, but I no longer pray for specific results and in any case I know that yanking the new season up from below the American border into this temperate just-right latitude would be well beyond my spiritual powers. Yearn as I might, I don't expect to get up one morning and find that all the trees in the park and on the hillside are suddenly green with fresh new leaves just because I want them to be. I do however take careful notice of their miniscule day-by-day changes.

Gombrich says perceiving is not the same as seeing, that perceiving is an active process that should more properly be called noticing. We look, he says, when our attention is aroused and only then do we notice that things aren't the way they were before, or as we expected them to be. Over a period of several days of intense observation from my eighth-floor balcony I thought I could detect an incremental thickening of the skeletal upper branches of the trees in the park. One morning there even seemed to be a decidedly purplish-pink colour in the crown of the great copper beech, so I went down on the elevator and out the front door and around the corner to the park and stood leaning against that massive trunk, staring upward. Sure enough, at the very tips of the highest branches little pointed red leaves were beginning to appear. I looked around and saw that tiny bright green blossoms were beginning to burst forth on the lower gray branches of the neighbouring maple tree.

As though to confirm my observations a rosy-headed house finch swooped down and landed on the back of one of the wooden park benches, trilled a few notes, and took off again.

Bibliography

William C. Agee, *Fairfield Porter*, The Parrish Art Museum, Southampton NY, 1993

Dore Ashton, *Artists on Art*, Pantheon Books, NY, 1985

W. H. Auden, *Collected Poems*, ed. Edward Mendelson, Faber & Faber, London, 1976

Peter Clothier, *David Hockney*, Abbeyville Press, New York, 1995

John Denison, *Casa Loma and the Man Who Built It*, Stoddart, Toronto, 1982

Umberto Eco, *History of Beauty*, Rizzoli, NY, 2004

James Elkins, *The Object Stares Back*, Simon & Schuster, NY, 1996

Lucian Freud, *Thoughts on Painting*, Encounter, #10, 1950

Michael Fried, *Art and Objecthood*, U. of Chicago Press, 1998

Ernst Gombrich, *Art and Illusion*, Princeton University Press, Princeton & Oxford, 1956

Clement Greenberg, *Art and Culture*, Beacon Press, 1961

Eric Hebborn, *Drawn To Trouble, Confessions of a Master Forger*, Random House, NY, 1991

Eric Hebborn, *The Art Forger's Handbook*, The Overlook Press, Woodstock, NY, 1997

Carolyn Heilbrun, *When Men Were the Only Models We Had*, University of Pennsylvania Press, 2001

Carolyn Heilbrun, *The Last Gift of Time, Life Beyond Sixty*, The Dial Press, NY, 1997

Carolyn Heilbrun, *Writing a Woman's Life*, Ballantine, Books, NY, 2002

David Hockney, *Secret Knowledge: Rediscovering the Lost Techniques of the Old Masters*, Viking, 2001

Thomas Hoving, *False Impressions: the Hunt for Big-Time Art Fakes*, Simon & Schuster, NY, 1996

William James, *The Varieties of Religious Experience*, Modern Library, Random House, NY, 1929

James King, *The Life of Margaret Laurence*, Alfred A. Knopf Canada, Toronto, 1997

Susan Kress, *Carolyn G. Heilbrun, Feminist in a Tenured Position*, University Press of Virginia, 1997

C. S. Lewis, *Surprised by Joy*, Harper Collins *Fount* reprint, UK, 1998

Lyall Powers, *Alien Heart, The Life and Work of Margaret Laurence*, U. of Manitoba Press, 2003

John Rattenbury, *A Living Architecture*, Warwick Press, 2001

Paul Tillich, *The Courage to Be*, Yale University Press, 1952

Karen Wilkin, *Giorgio Morandi*, Rizzoli, NY, 1997

The novels of Margaret Laurence

The novels of Carolyn Heilbrun

The novels of Mary Wesley